Jazz Party

a photo gallery of great jazz musicians

August House Publishers, Inc. • Little Rock, Arkansas

Jazz

a photo gallery of great jazz musicians

Party

al white

text edited by jim shacter

August House Publishers, Inc. • Little Rock, Arkansas

Published 2000 by August House Publishers, Inc., P.O. Box 3223,
Little Rock, Arkansas 72203, 501-372-5450.
Printed in Korea

Library of Congress Cataloging-in-Publication Data
White, Al 1928-
Jazz party: a photo gallery of great jazz musicians /
Al White; text edited by Jim Shacter.
    p. cm.
Includes index.
ISBN 0-87483-564-X (alk. paper)
1. Jazz musicians—Portraits. I. Shacter, James D. II. Title.

ML87.W55 2000
781.65'092'2—dc21
[B]   99-046072

The paper used in this publication meets the minimum
requirements of the American National Standard for
Information Sciences—Permanence of Paper for Printed Library
Materials, ANSI Z39.48-1984.

Photography: Al White
Text editor: Jim Shacter
Project director: Joy Freeman
Cover and book design: Buster Hall
Manuscript editor: Bill Jones
Editorial assistant: Jody McNeese

AUGUST HOUSE, INC.   PUBLISHERS   LITTLE ROCK

dedications

To my wife, Ann, who gave me love and understanding through the dark days

—A.W.

To Nancy, Joe, and Sara

—J.S.

contents

foreword

Al White has a bright, smiling face. It lights up all our jazz parties. He can be found, front and center, applauding like mad, urging us musicians on to ever-greater heights.

I met Al in New Orleans back in 1968. He and his wife, Ann, had attended our concert, which included Dick Hyman, Pee Wee Russell, Maxie Kaminsky, and others. My wife and I were having lunch at the Court of Two Sisters, when Al came over to our table and introduced himself as a jazz buff from Pine Bluff, Arkansas. He and Ann loved the concert and asked where they could find more of the same.

I suggested that they might come on out to Denver, where I had a booking at Elitch Gardens with the Ten Greats of Jazz, a band made up of Yank Lawson, Billy Butterfield, Peanuts Hucko, Lou McGarity, Cutty Cutshall, Bud Freeman, Ralph Sutton, Clancy Hayes, Morey Feld, and myself. Al knew them all, mostly by reputation, and he got very excited at the thought of hearing this all-star aggregation.

So, sure enough, Al White and his family showed up at Elitch's the following month and the rest is history. Loaded with his camera and plenty of film, Al wasted no time starting what turned into almost a second career of photographing jazz musicians.

He arrived at the next gathering, which became known as a "Jazz Party," put on by Dick Gibson in Aspen. Later parties moved to Vail, Colorado Springs, finally to Denver. At the last count, I believe Dick and Maddie Gibson gave over thirty parties, which grew larger every year.

Al attended most of these parties, as well as many others that sprang up around the country. He would arrive with several manila envelopes of photos ready to be autographed by the musicians. This has been Al's hobby, which turned into a marvelous collection of priceless photos and memorabilia, all signed by his devoted friends.

I know you'll enjoy this trip down jazz memory lane. I can't wait to get my copy!

BOB HAGGART

* * * * * *

Late in the summer of 1998, I asked Bob Haggart to write the foreword for this book. Bob and I had been close friends for years, and he sent the above paragraphs to me a few weeks later.

Traditional jazz lost a giant and one of its most beloved and highly respected figures when Hag died in December 1998. The news of his death came like a kick in the stomach, even though I knew he had been ill. Bob was one of the dearest, sweetest men I have ever known.

AL WHITE

preface

I've been very lucky taking pictures at jazz parties. I started photographing jazz musicians in 1968 and am still shooting more than thirty years later while working on this book. Happily, despite thousands of photos, no one in the audience has ever accused me of spoiling the music by snapping pictures during a performance.

My love of traditional jazz came from my mother, Mary Nell White, who was a jazz fan, played bluesy piano, and had a large record collection. I've played drums since the age of eight, and for a while thought vaguely about becoming a professional jazz drummer. My father, Alfred P. White, Sr., discouraged that idea firmly. So did Muggsy Spanier, who was playing at Nick's club in New York. Muggsy brought me down to earth: "Play drums for your own kicks. Don't make a business of it." Georg Brunis gave me the same advice: "Give up drums and be a lawyer and make more."

I ended up running a cotton company, which my family has been doing in Pine Bluff, Arkansas, since 1928. My father and his two brothers established the firm a few years earlier.

Bunny Berigan became my first jazz hero. I was nine or ten years old and talked my mother into buying every record we could find that featured him. In junior high school, I began to fill scrapbooks with photos of my favorite musicians and used every dime of my allowance to buy their records.

High school was spent at a military school in Columbia, Tennessee. I went to a Nashville orthodontist for periodic checkups on my braces, and on every trip I bought the latest Commodore records. Most of my friends had sports figures as heroes, but I worshipped the Condon gang. I hung out with other kids who loved jazz, and I played drums in the school orchestra and marching band. There was a good cornet player named Jim McEwan, and he and I liked to blast our way through the great duet by Ziggy Elman and Buddy Rich on Tommy Dorsey's record of "Well Git It." We thought we had it down pat.

In 1946, at the age of eighteen, I missed the draft by about two weeks and enrolled at the University of Arkansas. My classes started in January 1947. Pledging a fraternity, I was assigned to room with the president, a straitlaced war veteran. On my first night, I got drunk and threw up all over him from the top bunk. That escapade should have been a stern warning to me, but it took twenty-five years of hard drinking before I sought help. I haven't had a drink since March 1972.

Three jazz greats, all of whom had been heavy drinkers, played the leading roles in helping me stop drinking. Pee Wee Erwin and Lou McGarity planted the seed in my mind to take a good look at myself and seek assistance. Bob Haggart also gave me invaluable help.

My father suffered a stroke in 1948 while I was in college, and so I spent each fall buying cotton for our company. This procedure involved visually grading each bale and then measuring the average fiber length to determine the value of the bale. After going to school every spring and summer, I graduated in 1951 and then spent two years in the Army.

My parents gave me a small camera when I went to college, and my interest in photography started at that time. However, few pictures were taken until I married the girl next door, Ann Rowell, in 1956. Ann's grandfather had a complete photo studio in his basement, and he taught me about shooting, developing, and printing pictures.

Ann has given my life the stability it needed, and she stuck with me through the worst of the years of drinking. Although not a rabid jazz fan, she has great fondness for the musicians. More important, Ann has put up with my chasing after those guys like a blind dog in a meat house.

Milt Hinton does not claim to be a trained professional photographer, and neither do I. Since the mid-1930s, Milt as a professional musician has photographed many of the players with whom he has performed. Two books of his fine photos have been published, *Bass Line* and *Over Time*.

As a jazz fan, I have kept a pictorial record of the joy of knowing and hearing hundreds of marvelous musicians. I've collected more than 10,000 autographed pictures since 1968. I ask the musicians to sign one print of each photo for me, and I give one to them. I also ask many of them to autograph a print for my close friend Robert Nixon, a Pine Bluff ophthalmologist and fellow jazz nut.

I attended my first jazz party in 1970. That was seven years after a wealthy Denver businessman named Dick Gibson got the idea of engaging some of the world's finest jazz musicians to play at a popular vacation spot. He invited jazz fans from throughout the country to be paying guests. Gibson, a jazz lover since boyhood, scheduled a different combination of musicians to play each set. The grouping varied from one or two musicians to bands of a dozen or more instrumentalists.

Gibson and his family had moved to Denver from New York in 1960. He missed New York's jazz scene greatly and decided to do something about it. In 1963, during the three-day Labor Day weekend, Gibson put on his first jazz party, in Aspen, Colorado. It featured a band from Eddie Condon's club in New York. Wild Bill Davison fronted the group, which also included Cutty Cutshall, Edmond Hall, Ralph Sutton, Jack Lesberg, and Cliff Leeman. Alternating with the band was a trio led by Teddy Wilson, with Major Holley and Bert Dahlander.

Gibson's jazz party became an annual affair, and his roster of musicians grew every year. He was bringing more than forty players by the time Robert Nixon and I went to the 1970 party, in Vail, Colorado.

The photos in *Jazz Party* date back to the summer of 1968, when the Ten Greats of Jazz played at Elitch Gardens in Denver. This band, which became the World's Greatest Jazz Band, played the finest jazz I have ever heard. No wonder. The Ten Greats were Yank Lawson, Billy Butterfield, Cutty Cutshall, Lou McGarity, Peanuts Hucko, Bud Freeman, Ralph Sutton, Clancy Hayes, Bob Haggart, and Morey Feld.

Some of my most cherished pictures come from that 1968 gig. There's one of Hag with my ten-year-old son, Al III. Another shows Yank holding my daughter, Allyson, then seven.

For this book, I have chosen photos of my favorite musicians. How can so many great musicians be my "favorite" trumpet player, clarinetist, pianist, or drummer?

Because there is something unique about each one's playing that sets him apart from all the others.

Many jazz parties are called festivals, and new ones have been started continually through the years. Most of the pictures in this book were taken by me at parties held in a number of cities, including Atlanta; Denver; Indianapolis; Los Angeles; Minneapolis; St. Louis; San Diego; Aspen, Colorado Springs, and Vail, Colorado; Chautauqua, New York; Clearwater, Deerfield Beach, Pensacola, and St. Petersburg, Florida; Conneaut Lake, Pennsylvania; Kingsport, Tennessee; Menlo Park and Sacramento, California; Midland and Odessa, Texas; Waterloo Village (Stanhope), New Jersey; and Raleigh and Wilmington, North Carolina. History repeated itself in 1989, when Aspen again became the site of a jazz party.

Some parties follow Gibson's lead and feature musicians playing in combinations that change with each set. Audiences at other parties hear established bands whose members play together regularly throughout the year. By the late 1990s, jazz fans in the United States had their choice of about 150 annual jazz parties, some of which starred more than fifty musicians.

Dick Gibson died in 1998. As *The Mississippi Rag* observed in his obituary, jazz parties do much more for traditional jazz than simply provide entertainment for its devotees:

The [jazz party] concept, which essentially consisted of sophisticated jam sessions of musicians who may or may not have played together before, reinvigorated the jazz scene and led to the creation of jazz parties elsewhere. The Gibson parties also led to recording and club dates and jump-started many a career that had fallen into the doldrums due to lack of exposure rather than lack of talent....*

A.W.

* *The Mississippi Rag*, a matchless monthly publication devoted to traditional jazz, has a section that provides information about jazz parties in the United States and other countries. The *Rag* gives the name, date, place, and price of a party; the musicians and/or bands on the program; and the sponsor's name, address, and telephone number. Many parties also advertise in the *Rag*. The address of *The Mississippi Rag* is 9448 Lyndale Avenue South, Suite 120, Bloomington, Minnesota 55420.

Howard Alden

Howard's brilliant guitar playing, especially when he solos on up-tempo tunes, brings back memories of the great Charlie Christian. I first met Howard when he was touring with pianist Max Morath and doubling on banjo.

I always look forward to hearing Howard play guitar duets at jazz parties with such artists as Marty Grosz and Bucky Pizzarelli. In 1992, Howard switched from a six-string guitar to the seven-string instrument developed by George Van Eps. The two had recorded their first CD, *Thirteen Strings,* the previous year. Howard also made a unique and tasty guitar-bass CD with Jack Lesberg called *No Amps Allowed.* He is married to singer Terri Richards.

Howard and Dan Barrett, who are close friends, formed the Alden-Barrett Quintet, one of my favorite combos. Howard demonstrated his sharp sense of humor at the Wilmington, North Carolina, party when I asked him to inscribe a photo that I had taken of the two of them. He autographed it and, because Dan has a mustache, Howard drew one on his own lip.

The vigor of Howard's playing is reflected in this photo taken at the Indianapolis jazz party in 1994.

Not to be outdone by the mustache of his pal Dan Barrett, Howard drew one on his own lip at the party in Wilmington, North Carolina, in 1988.

Howard and Bucky Pizzarelli were swinging away on "Solo Flight" when I snapped them in Indianapolis in 1994. Before they started the tune, Howard facetiously told Bucky to watch out for the tricky third-trombone part.

Harry Allen

Harry, the bright young star of the tenor sax, was a fine third baseman who went to Rutgers on a baseball scholarship. Thank goodness he chose music.

I first heard Harry at Joe Boughton's Conneaut Lake party when he was in his 20s. Born in 1966, his playing and stage presence were remarkable for such a young musician. A few years later at Joe's party, Harry and Scott Hamilton, both of whom grew up in Rhode Island, played a rousing duet on "Crazy Rhythm." Bill Crow, the bass player and author of two fine jazz books, *Jazz Anecdotes* and *From Broadway to Birdland,* grabbed the mike and declared, "There must be something in the water in Rhode Island."

Before playing a duo set with Bucky Pizzarelli at one of the Odessa parties, Harry told the crowd that if it hadn't been for Bucky, he would not have been on that stage or any other. Bucky had promoted Harry and not only got gigs for him whenever he could, but also featured him on his own solo dates. Like Jim Galloway, Harry played with Bucky and Milt Hinton at private sessions after hours at the Odessa parties.

Harry continually fools with his tenor sax in an effort to make it sound better. He has just pulled the neck off the horn while posing with Joe Ascione. Ralph Sutton sits in the background. (Odessa, 1995)

Harry plays with the poise and ability of Bud Freeman, *left,* who was more than 60 years older. Bucky Pizzarelli and Ed Polcer can be seen behind them. (Conneaut Lake, 1988)

Bucky Pizzarelli accompanies Harry on one of the ballads that they play together so beautifully. Harry credits much of his success to Bucky, who promoted the younger musician's talents whenever he could. (Odessa, 1994)

Bill Allred

Bill took up the clarinet in sixth grade, but he didn't do too well with what he remembers as "all the squeaks and squawks." While reading an article on Tommy Dorsey in *Photoplay,* a movie magazine, Bill learned that Tommy and he had the same birthday, November 19. That was good enough for Bill. He took the clarinet back to the store, bought a trombone instead, and has been doing nicely with that instrument ever since.

Like most of the finest trombonists, Bill was influenced by Jack Teagarden. Once, while on tour in Texas, he was driving through the town of Vernon, where Jack was born and grew up. Bill looked all over for a memento of Jack and finally found a sporting goods store that sold him a Little League baseball shirt with "Vernon, Texas" on it. No one else appreciated the shirt, Bill said, but at least he had something from Jack's hometown.

At the Sacramento Jazz Jubilee in 1976, Bill sat in with the World's Greatest Jazz Band. He told me that he and George Masso made up the brass portion of the band's front line that night because Yank Lawson and Billy Butterfield had jubileed themselves out.

Bill performs at many jazz parties as leader of the Classic Jazz Band, composed of some of the top musicians of central Florida, where he lives. This band includes his son, John, also an excellent trombone player. Bill works a lot at Rosie O'Grady's, a popular jazz spot in Orlando, and plays many gigs for the Disney people in a group called the Rhythm Rascals.

This was my first photo of Bill, taken at the Wilmington party in 1982. I had listened to him on records for some time and was thrilled to finally hear him in a live performance.

Bill summed it all up when he inscribed a photo of Milt Hinton, *right,* and himself, "Fun with the Judge." (Indianapolis, 1987)

I love listening to Bill and Ken Peplowski, *left,* together in a traditional jazz band, and both hold their own with any of the more modern players as well. (Los Angeles, 1993)

John Allred

When John was ten years old, he decided to follow in the footsteps of his father and grandfather and be a jazz musician. Like his father, Bill, he is popular on trombone at jazz parties throughout the world. He was named for his grandfather, John William, who played banjo and piano.

I heard John play his first major jazz party in Indianapolis in 1988. He had been hired to take his father's place for the gig and was very nervous about it, but he came through like a champ, outplaying a lot of the old seasoned pros at the party.

I especially enjoy hearing John work with Allan Vaché, the excellent central Florida clarinetist. They have played together at Rosie O'Grady's in Orlando for a long time and at a number of the Odessa, Texas, parties. Allan has told me several times that John is his favorite trombonist.

Before a set at one of the parties in Odessa, Dan Barrett told the musicians he was going to call "Nagasaki" and that he and John would do a vocal duet on the old crowd pleaser. "Dan, I can't sing," John protested, adding that he didn't know the words either. Dan taught John the lyrics—and some clever alternate ones as well—in about fifteen minutes, and "Nagasaki" went over beautifully, sung at its customary breakneck tempo by the two ace trombonists.

John and Dan Barrett, *left,* do a fine vocal duet on "Nagasaki," even though John protests that he can't sing. (Odessa, 1996)

John has followed in the shoes of his father, Bill, as a top jazz trombonist. This youthful photo was taken at the Indianapolis party in 1988, where I heard John for the first time. He had never played a major party and was so nervous, Bill told me, that he could hardly make the gig.

By the time John played the Clearwater party in 1997, he had matured into a world-class performer. That's Bobby Gordon's clarinet in the foreground.

Tom Artin

Tom is a fine trombonist and the only top jazz musician I know of who has a Ph.D. He earned a doctorate in comparative literature at Princeton. Tom is also an excellent semiprofessional photographer.

I heard Tom for the first time in the mid-'70s, when he was at Condon's with Ed Polcer. Tom and Ed are both Princeton graduates and started playing together during their college days. Tom also worked a lot with Pee Wee Erwin at Condon's and played noon sessions called "Condon's Hot Lunch." He learned all the traditional trombone growls, grunts, smears, and swoops from Vic Dickenson and other masters.

Tom is a student of the great American composers of the '20s, '30s, and '40s. He loves to search out pretty ballads that haven't been played much, especially tunes by George Gershwin, Jerome Kern, Cole Porter, and Richard Rodgers, and feature them on his horn.

Tom and Pee Wee Erwin, *right,* were featured at Eddie Condon's club in New York in 1978. He shared the job of house trombonist with Vic Dickenson during this period.

Tom played at the Cornerstone in Metuchen, New Jersey, in 1982 with, *left to right,* Warren Vaché, Sr., Dick Sudhalter, Jane Jarvis, and Kenny Davern.

To Al, Best Wishes To You! Butch Miles

To Al, Best Wishes Tom Artin

When Tom, shown here with Butch Miles, *left,* leads a set, he not only chooses great old tunes, but also thinks up arrangements for them on the spot. (Wilmington, 1987)

Joe Ascione

Most of the fans who attend jazz parties have gray hair and worry about the future of this music. I have gray hair, but my concern about traditional jazz surviving in the years ahead diminishes when I hear Joe play the drums. Born in 1960, he is one of the youngest musicians who play these parties regularly.

I've played drums and listened to drummers since childhood, and Joe is one of the greatest I have ever heard. He plays the smoothest single-stroke roll on the snare drum with just his left hand while his right hand does tricks all over the drum set. That right hand knows all the stunts—and more—performed by every great drummer from Chick Webb to Buddy Rich.

Joe always has his eyes open for something new. When practicing the rudiments of drumming as a kid, he suspended a practice pad above his bed on a rope to enhance his touch. In 1996, he heard a Cuban drummer in New York use a device to play a cowbell with his right foot. Joe incorporated this apparatus into his drums by placing it next to his sock cymbal, so he could switch to the cowbell for Latin rhythms.

In 1998, at my 70th birthday party, Kenny Davern spotted a Chinese cymbal that was serving as a decoration. He flicked it and liked its sound. Kenny showed the cymbal to Joe, who also admired it. I gave him the cymbal, which became part of his drum set.

I enjoy hanging out with Joe's father, Vincent, at parties. No father could be prouder or more supportive of his son.

The 1992 Odessa party featured these brilliant drummers. After working up a sweat while playing a set, Joe shed his shirt and posed with, *left to right,* Jake Hanna and Jackie Williams. To celebrate his first visit to Texas, Joe put on a cowboy hat and hung a jalapeño pepper around his neck.

Joe's drums got lost by the airline en route to Fayetteville, Arkansas, in 1996 for a gig at my alma mater. He had to play my old drums, *above,* for the date at the University of Arkansas.

Despite his youth, Joe comes up with more innovative ideas than any other drummer I have ever heard.
Guys like him will keep classic jazz around for a long time. (Odessa, 1994)

Dan Barrett

Trombone is Dan's main instrument, and he plays it superbly. He doubles beautifully on trumpet or cornet. And he's also an excellent arranger who can write entire orchestrations without using a piano.

Dan's other credentials include music director of Arbors Records and of the Triangle Jazz Party in Kingsport, Tennessee. The Triangle party started after Steve Blades, a jazz fan who began playing trombone in seventh grade, heard Dan perform at a party in Wilmington, North Carolina. Steve introduced himself, and the two quickly became friends. When Steve got the idea of starting a jazz party, Dan immediately volunteered to help. He has guided the musical phase of the gig ever since.

Dan and his pal Howard Alden, who plays fantastic guitar, put together the ABQ, otherwise known as the Alden-Barrett Quintet. A great admirer of Rebecca Kilgore's singing, Dan wrote most of the arrangements and fronted the combo that played behind Becky on her *I Saw Stars* CD for Arbors.

A smile usually covers Dan's face. He frequently adds his trademark word of embellishment when announcing the name of a tune. Thus, "I Would Do Anything for You" becomes "I Would Do Anything for You, *Baby.*"

Dan is a top cornetist, in addition to being one of the finest trombonists I've ever heard. This musical genius can write a big-band arrangement with no piano, even while sitting in the back of a bus. (Indianapolis, 1994)

Dan and George Masso, *right,* became my favorite trombone duo after Lou McGarity and Cutty Cutshall died. Dan and George always delight the audience when they duet on "Get Out and Get Under the Moon," which Lou and Cutty used to feature. (Odessa, 1994)

I took this photo of Dan and Randy Sandke, *right,* in 1989 at the first of a series of great jazz parties in Aspen, Colorado, put on by Peter and Barbara Guy and Ralph and Sunnie Sutton.

Johnny Best

Johnny, a product of the Big Band Era, played trumpet in the bands of Les Brown, Charlie Barnet, Artie Shaw, Glenn Miller, and Benny Goodman during the '30s. and '40s. I first heard him at the Odessa jazz parties in the early '80s but had known about his playing in small bands of southern California from the '50s.

Johnny and Pee Wee Erwin were close friends and always enjoyed playing together. When Kenny Davern and Bob Wilber started their Soprano Summit combo, Johnny and Pee Wee said they were going to form a band and call it Brass Bottom.

In 1982, Johnny suffered a serious spinal injury when he fell from a high ladder on his avocado farm in southern California. He lay on the ground for about thirty hours before being found and has been in a wheelchair ever since. The accident did not dampen his spirit, however. Sitting in the chair, Johnny blasts away on his trumpet as though he were still standing up. Yank Lawson told me that Johnny tried to run the coyotes from the orchard at night by blowing high notes on his horn.

A genuinely friendly man, Johnny always joined the after-hours sets at Odessa in the upstairs party room. His exuberance had that wheelchair rocking.

Johnny gets a look of admiration from Ed Polcer, *right,* while soloing at the Odessa party in 1994. That's Jake Hanna on drums.

Two veterans of the Big Band Era, Johnny Mince, *left,* and Johnny Best, team up on a chorus at the 1979 Odessa gig.

Johnny and Ralph Sutton, *left,* have a drink together between sets. Johnny has been in a wheelchair since 1982 but seems to always have a smile on his face. (Odessa, 1994)

Keter Betts

Keter started out playing drums but switched to bass while in high school. He is an accomplished band bassist and excels especially when backing singers.

Keter accompanied Ella Fitzgerald on and off for twenty-four years and also worked with such vocalists as Chris Connor, Billy Eckstine, Roberta Flack, Dinah Washington, and Joe Williams. He played with guitarist Charlie Byrd and the bands of Earl Bostic and Woody Herman.

This warm, friendly, and humorous musician lives in Silver Spring, Maryland, near Washington, D.C., and enjoys playing for schoolchildren in the capital. He advises the youngsters that "Food is nourishment for the body, and music is nourishment for the mind." Giving his playing a personal touch, Keter tells them, "I'm not playing the bass. I'm playing *me*. That's me coming out of the bass."

Kids who learn something about jazz from someone as accomplished and caring as Keter can count themselves lucky.

As a kid, Keter admired the playing of Milt Hinton, *left,* so much that he wanted to sound just like him. Keter showed his feeling for Milt when inscribing the above photo. (Odessa, 1998)

Keter often signs my pictures "Bassically yours." I took this photo at the Indianapolis party in 1994, where he was a standout on his feature numbers.

That butterfly is out of sight, Bucky Pizzarelli

Before Keter and Bucky Pizzarelli, *left*, played a beautiful version of "Poor Butterfly" at the 1999 Kingsport party, he told the audience to watch the butterfly at the end of the tune. Hence his inscription.

Ruby Braff

Ruby produces a uniquely pretty sound on cornet. He and Dick Hyman have recorded cornet-piano duets for years, and their CDs offer some of the finest jazz around. So do those by Ruby and Dave McKenna.

Ruby's recordings also include the ones with guitarist George Barnes, supported by Wayne Wright on rhythm guitar and Michael Moore on bass. He has made excellent CDs as well with Scott Hamilton and a rhythm section. Another favorite of mine is the CD that Ruby made with Howard Alden and Jack Lesberg. He is a master of playing beautiful, soft jazz accompanied by only guitar and bass.

Bobby Rosengarden told me about the time Ruby and he played a gig in New York and discovered after they finished that a heavy snowstorm had hit the city. At 8 o'clock that morning, the equivalent of 2 a.m. for a working musician, Ruby woke Bobby up with a phone call and insisted—in vain—that they go to Central Park to build a snowman.

Jazz doesn't get much better than the duo of Ruby and Scott Hamilton, *right,* backed by a good rhythm section. They've made some superb recordings together, and hearing them at a jazz party is out of this world. (Minneapolis, 1987)

Ruby, shown with Benny Carter, *right,* produces a sound on the cornet that is difficult to describe except to say that it is compelling and beautiful. His notes range from a soft whisper to a clean, brassy shout. (Colorado Springs, 1978)

One of Ruby's most beautiful specialties is playing softly with guitar and bass accompaniment,
as Howard Alden and Jack Lesberg provided at the Minneapolis party in 1987.

John Bunch

A pleasant, soft-spoken man, John is strong and inventive at a piano keyboard. He has been musical director for Benny Goodman and Tony Bennett, but I like to hear him best in a Condon-type band. John was the house piano player at Condon's for a while in the early '80s. He also has played extensively in the Scott Hamilton Quintet.

John has done a lot of gigging and recording with Bucky Pizzarelli and Jay Leonhart in a combo called New York Swing. These three blend together beautifully and, backed by a drummer, form one of the tightest jazz groups I've ever heard.

Bob Haggart played with John and Bucky if Jay had another gig. Mat Domber recorded the trio for a fine Arbors CD called *Hag Leaps In*. Chances are you haven't heard "Big Noise from Winnetka" as it's done here, drumless with John's piano and Bucky's guitar sharing the track with Hag's bass. When they played the out chorus of an up-tempo tune, Hag liked to watch John's face light up.

John, seen here at the Odessa jazz party in 1988, is one of the true gentlemen of jazz, a fine piano player and one hell of a nice guy.

The look on Scott Hamilton's face shows what he thinks of John's playing. John has made some great recordings with Scott's quintet. (Conneaut Lake, 1987)

During a tour in the South that John made with Bob Haggart and Bucky Pizzarelli, *left and center,* the three did a record date for far below scale. As a result, Yank Lawson dubbed them The Three Turds. The photo was inscribed to my friend Robert Nixon. (Odessa, 1994)

Billy Butterfield

Billy got the fattest, most beautiful sound out of a trumpet that I've ever heard. In 1937, Bob Haggart and several other members of the Bob Crosby band heard Billy play. They made sure that Gil Rodin, the band's manager and lead alto sax player, hired him.

After leaving Crosby, Billy joined Artie Shaw. To me, Billy's solo on the Shaw record of "Stardust" ranks with Bix Beiderbecke's "Singin' the Blues" and Bunny Berigan's "I Can't Get Started."

The drinking escapades of Billy and Yank Lawson are legendary. Before Dick Gibson's 1971 jazz party, Ann told me not to come home unless I stopped drinking. Being the drunk that I was at the time, I got together with Yank and Billy. At about 2:30 a.m., we wound up in a room with a couple from Denver who had just been married.

My father had died the year before, and my mother had gone to the party with me. I took the whole group to our room after the police told us to quiet down, and Billy and I cracked open a bottle of vodka. Yank spotted my mother in bed and said jokingly, "Al, you and Billy go on to my room." My mother laughed and locked herself in the bathroom until I got everyone out of there.

Billy and Yank Lawson, *left,* were original members of the World's Greatest Jazz Band and two of the greatest trumpet players from the halcyon days of the Big Band Era. They are seen here in Memphis in 1978 during a gig by the WGJB.

Billy plays a solo while sitting in with the WGJB at a New York club in 1973. The other band members shown are, *left to right,* Bob Wilber, Bud Freeman, Bob Haggart, and Yank Lawson.

Dick Gibson, *left,* started the jazz party idea in 1963. He posed with Billy and my son, Al III, then ten years old, at Elitch Gardens in Denver in 1968.

Benny Carter

Benny is a giant of the alto sax. He and Johnny Hodges of Duke Ellington's band were the two major influences on this instrument during the '30s.

An extremely versatile musician, Benny also excels on trumpet, trombone, tenor sax, clarinet, and piano. In addition, he is a topflight arranger and composer, writing arrangements for Benny Goodman in the late '30s and working as a staff arranger for the BBC radio band in London.

I first heard Benny at Dick Gibson's jazz parties of the early '70s, where he always played both alto sax and trumpet. Benny is a very strong individual, but he cried like a baby at one of those parties when a friend told him that one of his old sidemen had died.

In 1989, Benny appeared on Marion McPartland's *Piano Jazz* radio program. They played duets on several of his best-known compositions, including two of my favorite tunes, "Blues in My Heart" and "When Lights Are Low," plus a lovely ballad, "Only Trust Your Heart."

Benny was one of five luminaries from the performing arts who were honored by President Clinton during the 1996 Kennedy Center Honors program on national television.

Benny Carter, shown with Alan Dawson on drums, is a giant of jazz. He plays not only beautiful trumpet and alto sax, his main instrument, but also ranks as a top arranger, composer, and band leader. (Colorado Springs, 1976)

Benny is one of the nicest and most approachable musicians I have ever met. This 1973 photo shows him soloing on alto sax at the world-famous Broadmoor Hotel in Colorado Springs.

To Al,
With thanks
& best wishes,
Bobby Hackett

To Al,
Sincerely
Benny Carter

While the rest of the band swings away at the 1973 Colorado Springs party, Benny and
Bobby Hackett work out what they're going to do next.

Dick Cary

Dick was a versatile musician who excelled on piano, trumpet, and alto horn. The latter has the nickname peck horn or, because its bell points straight up, rain catcher. Dick was associated with the Condon gang in the '40s and '50s, and Eddie Condon called it a valve bedpan.

Off and on during the '50s and '60s, Dick played piano for the Louis Armstrong All Stars. He loved to talk about Louis. I met Dick in 1976 when he played in Pine Bluff with Ralph Sutton, Jack Lesberg, and Gus Johnson at the wedding of Lyn Nixon, Jane and Robert's daughter. He stayed in my playroom and told some great stories about Brad Gowans, Billy Butterfield, and other musicians who had worked with Condon. Dick played the Conneaut Lake parties in the '80s.

He wrote a number of compositions. One of the most beautiful was "Ballad for Eddie," which Dick dedicated to tenor saxophonist Eddie Miller. Eddie recorded this tune shortly before Dick's death.

Dick got more beautiful jazz than anyone else from the alto horn, which Eddie Condon called a valve bedpan. This accomplished musician also was a top pianist and trumpet player. (Conneaut Lake, 1985)

Dick played all the Los Angeles Classic Jazz Festivals until his death in 1994. He held the piano chair with Louis Armstrong's All Stars during the '50s. (Los Angeles, 1991)

The taped-up spit valve on Dick's old alto trumpet can be seen in a photo taken at the 1985 Conneaut Lake party. He brought this horn and another trumpet to the 1976 wedding in Pine Bluff of Lyn Nixon, Jane and Robert's daughter. Dick played the wedding with Ralph Sutton, Jack Lesberg, and Gus Johnson.

Doc Cheatham

I wrote down these thoughts about Doc in June 1997 with tears in my eyes, having just learned that he had died eleven days before his 92nd birthday. This friendly, unassuming man was a powerhouse on the stand. He developed his strong chops playing lead trumpet with Cab Calloway, McKinney's Cotton Pickers, and a number of other big bands.

Doc also delighted audiences with his charmingly soft, warm vocals, especially when he cuddled up with "I Want a Little Girl." He sang four verses of "Manhattan," with lyrics that I didn't even know Lorenz Hart had written.

At a jazz party in Wilmington, North Carolina, the front line of one set consisted of Doc, George Masso, and Kenny Davern. They swung through a spirited "Jazz Band Ball," and a shout from Kenny accompanied the last note: "Wow, what a band!"

That same night, while Doc and I were having dinner together, our waitress complained about an upset stomach. "Young lady," said my companion, "I am Doctor Cheatham. Here is what you should do to take care of your stomach." And Doc told her, doubtless calling on the wisdom gained from all those years on the road.

Doc played with his trumpet pointed at the ceiling. This 1984 photo shows him at the Sweet Basil club in New York, where he performed on Sunday afternoons for the last fifteen years of his life.

Milt Hinton, *left,* and Doc starred with the great Cab Calloway band of the '30s and '40s. The curvature in Doc's upper lip shows the effect of seventy-five years of hard blowing. (Atlanta, 1995)

Doc played lead trumpet for Cab Calloway, and Trummy Young, *left,* was the featured trombonist with Jimmie Lunceford.
(Colorado Springs, 1978)

Greg Cohen

Greg, an excellent though comparatively young bass player, works hard at getting a true woody bass sound with as little amplification as possible. Many bassists crank their amp up as high as possible, which distorts the sound. Greg is the perfect bass player for a small group such as the Orphan Newsboys. Marty Grosz, who fronts the combo, praises Greg for providing "a pure, unadulterated pulse in this manic age of ricocheting decibels."

Greg grew up in Los Angeles but has worked on the East Coast for years. In 1989 and 1990, he served as musical director and arranger at the Thalia Theater in Hamburg, Germany. A CD that Greg made in 1996 shows off his talent as an arranger and composer. This recording, called *Low Down,* features a number of Duke Ellington compositions.

I enjoy sitting with Greg at jazz parties while listening to Dick Hyman or some other outstanding soloist, or a great combo—for example, New York Swing, made up of John Bunch, Bucky Pizzarelli, and Jay Leonhart. Greg provides an astute commentary about these superb players, enhancing my knowledge about them and their music.

The Orphan Newsboys, a fine quartet fronted by Marty Grosz, *left,* are anchored by Greg's bass. (Los Angeles, 1993)

Greg is one of my favorites of the relatively young bassists. He uses as little amplification as possible in producing a beautifully distinctive deep bass sound. (Atlanta, 1994)

This photo, taken at the New Jersey Jazz Society in Hoboken in 1995, shows Greg trading fours with Kenny Davern, *right.* The expression on Jake Hanna's face reflects his appreciation of Greg's playing.

Al Cohn

Al played tenor sax in several of the big bands during the '40s, including those of Georgie Auld, Buddy Rich, Woody Herman, and Artie Shaw. He also was a fine jazz composer and arranger, writing material for such television programs of the '50s as the *Hit Parade* and Steve Allen's *Tonight Show*.

In the late '50s, Al and Zoot Sims formed a quintet to play a gig at the Half Note Club in New York. They worked together off and on for the rest of their lives. Both had been members of the Four Brothers sax team of Herman's band in the late '40s.

I first heard Al play at Dick Gibson's parties of the early '70s, and the last time was at a jazz party in Wilmington, North Carolina, in 1982. He and Flip Phillips played some great tenor sax duets at that party, and pianist Dave Frishberg performed several of Al's tunes.

Almost every time I asked Al to inscribe a photo for me, he wrote, "From one music lover to another."

Al, a fine straight-ahead tenor sax man from the Big Band Era, was also a top arranger and composer. Trombonist Jimmy Knepper stood to his left in this shot of Al taking a solo. (Colorado Springs, 1978)

Johnny Mince, another veteran of the big bands, watches Al approvingly. Oliver Jackson is on drums. When Al autographed my photos, he almost always wrote, "From one music lover to another." (Colorado Springs, 1974)

To Al,
all the best,
Al Cohn

Al, shown here with Jon Faddis at Colorado Springs in 1978, was a master of the
deep-sounding tenor sax style that started with Coleman Hawkins in the '20s.

Jackie Coon

Jackie plays only the flugelhorn now, but in his younger days he played cornet with Jack Teagarden, Nappy Lamare, Ray Bauduc, Eddie Miller, and other jazz stars. Jackie is one of the greatest natural talents I have ever heard, and he's perfect in the small-band setting that I love so much. In addition to being a great brass player, Jackie is a top jazz singer. He knows the words to a lot of old standards that I didn't even know had lyrics.

A friendly, lovable guy who is fun to be around, Jackie has spent almost his entire career working in clubs on the West Coast and for Disney. He and banjoist Eddie Erickson have an act that brings cheers from jazz party crowds.

At the 1996 Triangle party in Kingsport, Tennessee, Jackie was asked to lecture and play the flugelhorn for a group of high school students. Dan Barrett gave him his cornet to show the kids the difference between the two instruments. Unfortunately, Dan forgot to tell Jackie that there was a trick to opening the cornet case. Jackie did a fine job talking to the kids and playing for them. But when the time came to demonstrate the difference between a flugelhorn and a cornet, all he could say was, "I know there's a cornet in here someplace."

Jackie is an entertaining jazz singer as well as a top brass player. He and banjo player Eddie Erickson perform vocal and instrumental duets that always bring down the house. (Los Angeles, 1991)

Just before I snapped this photo, Jackie and Ralph Sutton, *left,* played a fine duet. Jazz writer Floyd Levin stands in front of them. (Los Angeles, 1996)

Jackie does all the tricks on his flugelhorn that a good trumpet player can do on a trumpet. Yank Lawson used to introduce him as "Citizen Coon." They were great poker-playing pals. (Los Angeles, 1953)

Jim Cullum

In 1962, the father-and-son team of Jim Cullum, Sr., on clarinet and Jim Cullum, Jr., on cornet formed the Happy Jazz Band. The group became the Jim Cullum Jazz Band following the death of Jim, Sr., in 1973. This marvelous band, propelled by the leader's powerful cornet, plays at The Landing, a club owned by Jim on the Riverwalk in San Antonio.

Like Turk Murphy, Jim has always had a well-rehearsed band. It has recorded many tasty albums, including a number of live radio broadcasts from The Landing. These shows have highlighted such historic jazz figures as Earl Hines, Bob Crosby's Bob Cats, and Jack Teagarden. Jim brought in Dick Hyman for the Hines show and Bob Haggart for the Crosby broadcast. My favorite was the Teagarden show, which starred Dan Barrett and Bob Havens on trombone, as well as Jack's sister, Norma Teagarden, on piano.

Jim's band plays at some jazz parties every year. It has been the highlight of Summit Jazz since 1983. Juanita Greenwood and Alan Frederickson put on this party in Denver, and they started an annual series of Swinging Jazz Concerts there in 1997.

The Cullum repertoire includes many tunes by Louis Armstrong, Jelly Roll Morton, King Oliver, and other legendary artists. The charts are written by pianist John Sheridan. There's a section about him in this book.

The other sidemen in the Cullum band are also world-class musicians. Photos of them appear on pages 42 and 43.

Driven by the leader's powerful cornet, the peerless Jim Cullum Jazz Band plays at The Landing, a club in San Antonio. Jim started his career with his father, Jim, Sr., a clarinetist from the Big Band Era. (Pensacola, 1990)

Two great brass players got together when Doc Severinson, *left,* dropped in to hear Jim's band play at a trade show in Chicago in 1987.

Merrill Harris, a friend from Jackson, Mississippi, who attended many jazz parties, invited Ann and me to hear the Cullum band play a gig there after it had worked Mardi Gras in 1975. In those days, Jim brought a trumpet, a cornet, and a flugelhorn, *above,* to work each night.

Jim Cullum's Sidemen

Don Mopsick brings his bass to the front of the stand and knocks out the audience when he sings wistfully about the day "When the Bass Players Take Over the World." He has been on bass with the Cullum band since Jack Wyatt died. (St. Louis, 1992)

Mike Pittsley gets a warm sound out of his trombone that reminds me of an old favorite of mine, Cutty Cutshall. He's shown here with Jim Cullum at the 1987 Chicago trade show where I took the photo of Jim and Doc Severinson. Mike was preceded in the band by Eddie Hubble, one of my all-time favorites, and the versatile Randy Reinhart, who doubles on trumpet.

Ed Torres is a pulsating, underrated drummer whose light touch fits the Cullum group perfectly. This shot shows the little Chinese tom-tom that he uses so effectively with his Ray Bauduc-type wood blocks and cow bells. I love to hear Ed, using brushes on just snare drum and sock cymbal, when he accompanies John Sheridan out on the patio at The Landing. (St. Louis, 1992)

Evan Christopher was packing his clarinet and other gear when I snapped this photo after a concert by the Cullum band. Edmond Hall was his hero, and you can hear Edmond in his playing. Evan followed Bobby Gordon, Allan Vaché, and Brian Ogilvie as Jim's clarinetist. (Little Rock, 1997)

Howard Elkins lays down driving rhythm on guitar and banjo for the Jim Cullum Jazz Band. He's also a fine vocalist. Howard was doing the vocal on the Louis Armstrong classic "S.O.L. Blues" when I took this photo at the 1986 Mid-America Jazz Festival in St. Louis.

Ron Hockett succeeded Evan Christopher with Jim after retiring in 1998 from a career playing clarinet and alto sax in the U.S. Marine Band. Years ago, he and John Sheridan, then a member of the U.S. Navy Band, became friends while moonlighting on club dates in Washington. Ron played several jazz parties during his final years with the Marine Band. (Odessa, 1988)

Cutty Cutshall

Cutty played trombone in the band at Eddie Condon's when I began going to the club in 1952. He was much nicer to me, a twenty-four-year-old Army second lieutenant, than any of the other musicians. Between sets, Cutty gave me the names of the tunes just played, told me about the other players, and reminisced about his background as the son of a Pennsylvania coal miner. I loved Cutty's sound on his horn, pretty and deep-throated.

I didn't see Cutty again until that wonderful weekend in 1968 at Elitch Gardens in Denver, when he was one of the Ten Greats of Jazz. Cutty kept several packages of chewing gum in his trombone case to prevent his mouth from getting dry. On the first night at Elitch's, Dick Gibson's little boy carefully opened each package, removed every stick of gum, and replaced the wrappings in the case. Janey Nixon came to Cutty's rescue with some supplementary gum.

My biggest thrill that night came when Clancy Hayes sang "Rose of Washington Square," with Cutty playing a beautiful obbligato part behind him and then blowing a bluesy solo. I will never forget the warmth of Cutty's friendship and of the sound on his trombone.

Cutty and Lou McGarity, *right,* posed with me when the Ten Greats of Jazz played at Elitch Gardens in Denver in 1968. They were my favorite trombonists, and I treasure this photo above all others. It appears on the jacket of *Jazz Party.*

Cutty, shown with Yank Lawson, Bob Haggart, and Morey Feld, *left to right,* was playing behind Clancy Hayes's vocal on "Rose of Washington Square" when this shot was taken. (Denver, 1968)

Dick Gibson's young son swiped the chewing gum that Cutty carried in his trombone case to keep his mouth moist. Janey Nixon provided an emergency supply, and Cutty wasted no time using it. (Denver, 1968)

Kenny Davern

I first heard Kenny's clarinet on an LP by the Dixie Rebels, led by someone named Big Jeb Dooley. Big Jeb turned out to be Pee Wee Erwin, and the other members of the band weren't bad either—Lou McGarity, Johnny Varro, Milt Hinton, and Cliff Leeman. The two records made by the Dixie Rebels, in 1959 and 1961, still sound as fresh and exciting as ever.

To me, Kenny is one of the finest clarinet players to come along. He has a remarkable range on his instrument. Kenny can sustain notes higher than any other clarinetist, and those notes sound great and fit the tune being played, especially the end of a number. At a 1997 party, he and Ralph Sutton played a duet on "Comes Love" in which Kenny never left the lower register.

Both Kenny and Ralph were hired by Jack Teagarden when they were in their teens. Kenny loves the playing of Pee Wee Russell but does not just imitate him. His sound is uniquely his own.

Kenny detests poor sound systems and does not hesitate to share his views about such deficiencies. His acerbic remarks have delighted many jazz party audiences.

Robert Nixon's wife, Janey, a prim and proper lady, became embarrassed and turned bright red at an off-color story told by Kenny at one of the Odessa parties. "Janey," Kenny advised her, "the way to get over that is to look in the mirror each morning and yell, 'Shit!'"

Kenny was playing the straight soprano sax and Bob Wilber, *right,* the curved version of the instrument when I took this photo at the birth of Soprano Summit. Ray Brown is on bass. Dick Gibson asked Kenny and Bob to play a duet, and they chose Duke Ellington's "The Mooche." The audience went wild, and the rest is history. (Colorado Springs, 1973)

Kenny coaxes high notes out of a clarinet that are not actually on the horn, and he plays slow ballads more beautifully than any other clarinetist I have ever heard. He was devoted to Pee Wee Russell and owns Pee Wee's clarinet and one of his famous paintings. But like Pee Wee, Kenny is his own man when he plays. (Pensacola, 1990)

Pee Wee Erwin, *left,* and Kenny got together with Robert Nixon, *right,* and me at the Odessa party in 1974. When Kenny and Bob Wilber started Soprano Summit, Pee Wee complained that his two favorite clarinetists were playing "fish horns."

Wild Bill Davison

In 1952, with my first Army weekend pass, I went straight from Fort Devens, Massachusetts, to Eddie Condon's club and perched at Wild Bill's feet. He had a bass tom-tom in front of him that served as a table for his ashtray and drinks. After a particularly rousing number, Bill would yell, "Whiskey!" He had a crusty exterior but was a marshmallow inside.

Bill played at my first Odessa, Texas, jazz party, in May 1972. I had stopped drinking two months earlier, but I bought him a bottle of scotch. Bill hid the whiskey from his wife, Anne, who is one of the nicest ladies I've ever met. She kept Bill going through the years and blasting away on his cornet longer than anyone thought he would.

In 1971, he performed at a Community Concert in Pine Bluff with Barney Bigard, Art Hodes, and Eddie Condon. Bill was very sweet to my eleven-year-old daughter, Allyson. I played my drums with him while my mother accompanied us on our piano. Early the next morning, as I drove Bill and Eddie to their motel, Bill kept saying, "Fuck you, Condon." Eddie turned to me and replied, "Now do you see why we call him wild?" Many stories about Bill's wildness appear in his entertaining biography, *The Wildest One*, by Hal Willard.

Wild Bill has a disciple, cornetist Tom Saunders. Tom has carried on Bill's music at jazz parties, just as Bob Wilber has done with Sidney Bechet's. There's a section on Tommy in this book.

Wild Bill and my daughter, Allyson, posed together at the 1982 Mid-America Jazz Festival in St. Louis. She is holding a photo of them taken in my gun room in 1971, when Allyson was eleven years old. Bill was playing a gig in Pine Bluff with a group led by Art Hodes.

This photo captures the exuberant drive of Bill's cornet when he was almost eighty. That's Milt Hinton on bass. (St. Louis, 1982)

Bill blasts away at the 1972 Odessa party with, *left to right,* Kenny Davern, Jack Lesberg, Flip Phillips, and Cliff Leeman.

Vic Dickenson

It's not too hard to recognize the unique sound that Vic got from his trombone. Those funny growls and low notes reflect the man's beautiful sense of humor. I've never heard anyone, except perhaps Jack Teagarden, play the blues like Vic. He composed several lovely tunes, including "Constantly" and "I'll Try."

During the period that Vic was a member of the World's Greatest Jazz Band, Bob Haggart wrote several tunes to commemorate various spots where the group had played. One of them was "Frog and Nightgown," named for a club in Raleigh, North Carolina, and featuring Vic's humorous growls. Yank Lawson would introduce the tune and tell the audience, "Vic is going to be the frog, and I guess I'll be the nightgown." The back-and-forth between trombone and trumpet on the band's *Century Plaza* record is a joy to hear.

In 1978, Vic played at a Christmas jazz party in Denver put on by two rabid fans, Connie Roscoe and Dick Weyrich. The other musicians were Pee Wee Erwin, Peanuts Hucko, Ralph Sutton, and Gus Johnson. My hotel room was next to Vic's, and I hung out with him and Pee Wee. When I offered to buy Vic a drink, he said "Ding." I later learned that Ding was his nickname among the musicians. When he referred to something as "Ding Ding," it was extra special. Manfred Selchow's excellent biography of Vic is called *Ding! Ding!*

Vic's unique style featured little grunts, groans, and growls that were always in good taste and in just the right places. He's using his hand as a mute in this photo, and his old buddy Gus Johnson can barely be seen smiling behind him at the drums, *right*. (Denver, 1974)

Vic could put his horn on the floor and deliver the most pleasing jazz vocals. The other musicians in the performance shown above included Warren Vaché, *left*. (Great Gorge, New Jersey, 1978)

Two of the greatest bassists and trombonists—Jack Lesberg, Milt Hinton, Vic Dickenson, and George Masso, *left to right*—smiled for the camera one night at Condon's in 1978.

George Duvivier

George was one of the last bass players in Jimmie Lunceford's great band of the late '30s and early '40s. I first heard him at the Gibson party in Colorado Springs after he had driven his big Cadillac from New York with his bass lying across the back seat.

George played with Kenny Davern and Bob Wilber in the first recording session of Soprano Summit, and the three of them also performed in Pine Bluff. I've known few men as friendly as George. He once owned a bar in New York, and his personality must have made it a popular spot. He told me that anyone who came into his place with the idea of outdrinking him made a big mistake, because of his huge capacity.

A sound buff, George had state-of-the-art equipment in his apartment. The manufacturer warned that it should not be played too loudly, but George figured, "What the hell, it's my equipment." So he cranked it up and cracked the ceiling.

Soprano Summit at, in my opinion, its best: Kenny Davern, Marty Grosz, Connie Kay, Bob Wilber, and George Duvivier, *left to right.* This was one of the finest small bands I have ever heard, and George's bass played an integral role in it. (Pine Bluff, 1975)

George was one of the most widely respected and popular jazz musicians in New York from the early '40s until his untimely death in 1985. (Odessa, 1979)

The Soprano Summit musicians flew back to New York after playing in Pine Bluff in 1975. The flight was unusual for George, who thought nothing of driving 2,000 miles to a gig with his 250-year-old bass in the back seat. At the Little Rock airport I snapped Connie, George, Kenny, Bob, Marty, and my friend Robert Nixon, *left to right*.

Peter Ecklund

Peter plays trumpet and cornet and is co-leader with Marty Grosz of the Orphan Newsboys. I especially like his work with Bobby Gordon, the combo's clarinet player.

The Orphan Newsboys played in Pine Bluff for the opening of the city's Arts and Science Center. Peter is very thin, and he surprised me with the power he gets from his horn. He had a guitar with him and practiced on it every day.

Peter blew all the bugle calls for *The Civil War,* the renowned Ken Burns television series. I have collected Civil War relics for years and came across two old brass mouthpieces. They fascinated Peter so much that I gave them to him. He took them to an expert in New York, who recognized one as a bugle mouthpiece and the other as part of a rare E-flat horn.

Peter played lead trumpet for Vince Giordano's Nighthawks for several years. He also is an accomplished arranger and composer.

I gave Peter a copy of this photo, taken at the Conneaut Lake, Pennsylvania, party in 1988. It was published in a French jazz magazine during one of his gigs over there. Peter, with Marty Grosz, is co-leader of the Orphan Newsboys.

Peter got top grades from fellow whistler Bob Haggart, *right,* for both his whistling and his trumpet and cornet playing. (Pensacola, 1990)

Bobby Gordon

Peter Ecklund

Bob Havens

Bobby Gordon, *left,* and Bob Havens flanked Peter on this front line at Conneaut Lake in 1989. Peter played a beautiful tune at the 1998 Atlanta party based on a two-bar phrase by Bix Beiderbecke. He gave it the title "New Bix," which Marty Grosz said sounded like a detergent.

Herb Ellis

Herb and his guitar have backed Oscar Peterson, Ella Fitzgerald, and other top jazz soloists. His career began in the '40s, when he played in the bands of Jimmy Dorsey, Glen Gray, and Russ Morgan.

For six years, Herb and Ray Brown worked in the Oscar Peterson Trio. Herb later joined forces with Joe Pass, and the two of them got together with Charlie Byrd to form a trio, appropriately called the Great Guitars. He spent most of the '50s and '60s as a television studio musician in Hollywood.

Herb grew up in Texas and always enjoyed playing the Odessa jazz parties. O.A. (Jim) Fulcher, an Odessa physician who started that party in 1964, liked to schedule two-guitar sets featuring Herb and Bucky Pizzarelli. When the crowd got too noisy, he would yell, "Shut up, you oil-field sons of bitches, and listen to some pretty music!"

I went with Herb and Bucky when they played at one of the Odessa schools. The amplifier conked out and the two master guitarists had to play acoustically for the kids. You could have heard a pin drop.

Contrary to their expressions, Herb and Bucky Pizzarelli, *left,* got a big kick playing an afternoon gig at a local school while performing at the 1977 Odessa party.

Herb did some of his finest work during his six years in the Oscar Peterson Trio, which also starred Ray Brown on bass. (Colorado Springs, 1973)

Four world-class guitarists, Bucky Pizzarelli, Howard Alden, Herb Ellis, and Billy Bauer, *left to right,* dazzled the audience with a set at the 1995 March of Jazz in Deerfield Beach, celebrating Flip Phillips' 80th birthday.

Eddie Erickson

Eddie combines the talents of a master banjo and guitar player and an incredible entertainer. The banjo, a difficult instrument, becomes a thing of beauty in his hands. He is known at jazz parties for his duo acts with banjoist-guitarist-trombonist Bill Dendle and flugelhornist Jackie Coon.

The great banjo playing and comic patter of Eddie and Bill always bring wild applause from the audience. They have worked out routines for such jazz classics as Fats Waller's "Handful of Keys" that are remarkable for two banjos.

Like Marty Grosz, Eddie has the ability to take whatever is going on in the room where he is performing—whether it centers on the musicians, the audience, or the room itself—and make it funny. One of his specialties is a hilarious fractured-French version of "C'est Si Bon."

For jazz to be entertaining, it should be fun. Eddie contributes much more than his share.

Eddie and Jackie Coon, *left,* shown with Dave Stone on bass, have worked out several routines that keep the fun in jazz. They combine fine musicianship with great humor. (Clearwater, 1997)

These two top singers, Becky Kilgore and Eddie, had never performed together until the 1995 Triangle party in Kingsport. They worked out several on-the-spot duets that wowed the audience.

Eddie asked me to take a photo of him with two of his heroes, Rick Fay and Milt Hinton, *left and center*. His face lit up when I gave him a copy. (Kingsport, 1995)

Pee Wee Erwin

Pee Wee will always be in my thoughts as a gentle man who took the time to try to help an unknown jazz fan.

In September 1971, I went to the Gibson jazz party in Colorado Springs with my mother and Robert and Jane Nixon. This was the worst of my drinking period, and Ann had told me not to come home unless I did something to help myself.

As soon as Pee Wee finished his first set at that party, I rushed backstage to meet him. Gushing about his trumpet playing, I was as drunk as a billy goat and must have made a horrible impression. Lucky for me, Pee Wee was a recovering alcoholic. During the weekend, he somehow made me realize I needed help. Pee Wee forced me to look at myself with his frank account of how his own drinking had ruined his career with a great band. He had booked this band, which included Kenny Davern and Johnny Varro, throughout the country.

I did not stop drinking until March 19, 1972, but Pee Wee planted the seed that saved me. Never have I known a kinder person.

In 1978, I asked Pee Wee to bring a band to Pine Bluff for my 50th birthday party. The other musicians were Warren Vaché, Jr., Eddie Hubble, Kenny Davern, Bob Wilber, Marty Napoleon, Milt Hinton, and Cliff Leeman.

With the help of Merrill Harris, a jazz fan from Jackson, Mississippi, I also got the band a gig there. While driving down to Jackson, we stopped for gas in Dumas, Arkansas. When Pee Wee realized where we were, he stood in the middle of the street with his horn and blew the greatest "Ding Dong Daddy from Dumas" I've ever heard. I'll never forget the look on the face of the lady who ran the gas station.

The touching story of Pee Wee's life, *This Horn for Hire,* was written by Warren Vaché, Sr.

The trumpets of Pee Wee and Doc Cheatham led the way in a set at the Colorado Springs party in 1978. The musicians included, left to right, Kenny Davern, Major Holley, Bob Wilber, Pee Wee, Doc, Scott Hamilton, Roy Williams, and Eddie Hubble. Williams lost his luggage on the flight from England and played the entire party in this outfit.

Like all jazz musicians, Pee Wee loved Louis Armstrong. He asked me to take this photo of Louis's widow, Lucille, and himself. (Colorado Springs, 1975)

This is a favorite picture of a favorite person. I took it during a jazz party put on by Connie Roscoe and Dick Weyrich. The band consisted of Pee Wee, Vic Dickenson, Peanuts Hucko, Ralph Sutton, and Gus Johnson. (Denver, 1974)

Here's Pee Wee in Dumas, Arkansas, in 1978 after playing "Ding Dong Daddy from Dumas" in the street. He had recently stopped smoking and was chewing tobacco. "Al, I'm in trouble," Pee Wee said in the high wind. "I can't spit."

Rick Fay

Rick was not only a standout musician on all the reed instruments, chiefly tenor sax, but also got a lot of laughs as an outstanding comedian. He always brought down the house with "Teenie Weenie Blues," which he played on a toy whistle shaped like a tiny Oscar Mayer hot dog.

Throughout most of his career, Rick worked for the Disney empire. He started at Disneyland in California and then performed for thirty years at Disney World in Florida, where he led the famous Pearly Band. Dan Barrett introduced me to him at the Los Angeles Jazz Classic and related that Rick had helped him greatly to get gigs as a young musician. Rick also played at the March of Jazz, the Triangle Jazz Party, the Sacramento Jazz Jubilee, and the Suncoast Dixieland Jazz Classic.

Recording extensively for Arbors as both leader and sideman, Rick made CDs, including *Sax-O-Poem* and *Words Among the Reeds,* that feature his original poetry with jazz background. He chats about his life as a jazz artist and his thoughts covering musicians from Bix Beiderbecke to the present.

Rick wore a jacket with the Arbors Records logo at the 1997 March of Jazz in Clearwater. Had it not been for Rick, there probably wouldn't have been an Arbors. He planted the seed with Mat and Rachel Domber to establish the company.

Rick's main instrument was tenor sax, but he also excelled on clarinet, *above,* and soprano sax. He played all three and recited original poetry on CDs that feature top sidemen. (Kingsport, 1994)

An excellent judge of talent, Rick boosted the careers of many younger musicians, including Dan Barrett, *right.* (St. Petersburg, 1994)

Carl Fontana

Carl, a fine trombonist from Monroe, Louisiana, started his career at the age of fifteen with a band in the cotton-growing area where I have worked all my life. The group was led by his father, Callie Fontana, who played tenor sax and violin.

Carl was one of Dick Gibson's favorite trombone players and worked all the early Gibson jazz parties of the '70s and also the first Odessa parties. After the death of Cutty Cutshall, Carl replaced him in the World's Greatest Jazz Band and played with that group through the '70s. He has lived in Las Vegas for years and has played in many pit bands there in addition to traveling throughout the world doing jazz parties.

To Carl, pianist Lou Stein was always Lou Steinway. The two of them played golf with trombonist Kai Winding, who frequently hooked the ball. Carl called him Captain Hook and made up a little blues called Steinway, Nobbins, and Hook. It was too raunchy to be sung in public.

Carl was playing Lou McGarity's old trombone when I took this photo. The two had worked together in the World's Greatest Jazz Band. Carl loved Lou's playing, but he hated this small-bore horn and called it a peashooter. He quipped that Lou had not left any good notes in it. That's Ray Mosca on drums. (Odessa, 1983)

Gus Johnson, *left,* was Carl's best friend in the WGJB, They called each other "catfish" because of their mutual fondness for this dish. (Odessa, 1985)

One of the sets at the 1975 Odessa party featured, *left to right,* Jack Lesberg, Kenny Davern, Ed Polcer, and Carl Fontana.

Bud Freeman

Early in his career, Bud developed a distinctive and easily identifiable sound on tenor sax. He had a huge ego, but he played so well that everyone put up with it. Bud once cornered Kenny Davern after a gig and talked about himself for a couple of hours. When Kenny thought he had finally wound down, Bud asked, "Now, Kenny, what do *you* think of me?"

Bud played at many of the Conneaut Lake jazz parties. On the stand, he spent about as much time talking about the funny things that had happened to him through the years as he did playing. He and Eddie Miller, another great tenor player, appeared together at several of these gigs. Bud was using a sax that Eddie had "sold" him about twenty years earlier but for which he had never paid. Bud gave Eddie an elaborate ten-minute introduction during one set and then asked, "Eddie, what have you been saying about *me* lately?"

Bud wrote an autobiography called *Crazeology* with Robert Wolf, plus two books of anecdotes, many of them hilarious, *You Don't Look Like a Musician* and *if you know of a better life!* His stories cover his early career as a member of the Austin High Gang of Chicago and as a sideman with such leaders as Tommy Dorsey and Benny Goodman, and his later years as a star soloist and then as a charter member of the World's Greatest Jazz Band.

When Bud lay dying in a Chicago nursing home, Yank Lawson visited him one day. "Yank, I'm worth several million," Bud told him. "Bud, just loan me one million," Yank replied.

This shot of Bud with Yank Lawson and Bob Haggart, *left to right,* at the 1986 Indianapolis party showed up in a wonderful little book called *Crazeology,* his autobiography.

Bud was a true giant of jazz. I especially enjoyed him at the Conneaut Lake party because it was so informal that Bud spent about as much time telling stories about his life as he did playing. (Conneaut Lake, 1985)

Bud takes a solo during a performance by the band that became the World's Greatest Jazz Band. The group included, *left to right,* Ralph Sutton, Clancy Hayes, Peanuts Hucko, and Bob Haggart. (Denver, 1968)

Dave Frishberg

Dave is not only a wonderful jazz pianist, but also a clever lyricist and composer. He has turned out a number of CDs that feature him singing and playing his own witty songs, including "My Attorney Bernie," "Quality Time," and "Van Lingle Mungo."

I first heard Dave at the jazz party in Wilmington, North Carolina, in 1989. Particularly notable was a solo set in which he played a medley of seldom-heard tunes by Johnny Hodges, such as "Star-Crossed Lovers," "Squatty Roo," and "The Jeep Is Jumpin'." Dave also sang a clever blues based on the names of great old-time baseball players.

Dave works regularly with vocalist Becky Kilgore at the Heathman Hotel in Portland, Oregon, where both live. They sound particularly good because they have worked as a duo so much. Becky and Dave perform a lot of their own arrangements of fine songs that have not been played to death through the years. Their CDs together include *Looking at You* and *Not a Care in the World*.

Dave has written many clever songs that he sings to his own piano accompaniment. I especially like "I Want to Be a Sideman." (Clearwater, 1996)

Dave and Gerry Wiggins, *left,* another fine pianist, seem to be having a thoughtful discussion at the Triangle party. (Kingsport, 1995)

EXCUSE ME, AL — I'M MISSING AN F# ~

Dave Frishberg

When I asked Dave to autograph this photo, I mentioned that he always looks so serious in my shots of him at the piano. "Jazz," he replied, "is a serious business." (Clearwater, 1997)

Jim Galloway

Jim is a master of the soprano sax. He has a distinctive little growl on the horn that is his trademark and isn't used by most players. Jim doesn't overuse the growl, but always plays it in just the right spot. He doubles on baritone sax and likes to take an obscure song, such as "Yes, We Have No Bananas," and play it on the baritone as a beautiful slow ballad.

Jim immigrated to Canada from Scotland in 1964 and speaks with a lovely Scottish accent. He lives near Toronto and is very active on the Canadian jazz scene. Jim's Wee Big Band started performing in 1979 and recorded a Sackville CD called *Kansas City Nights.* He also made a Christmas album and several other recordings with Ralph Sutton, Milt Hinton, and Gus Johnson.

The high point of the Odessa parties for me came when a group of jazz fans from California rented a room and invited several other people from the audience to come up after each evening's performance. Milt would bring his bass, Bucky Pizzarelli would have his guitar, and Jim and perhaps two other horn players would be there. It was magic to hear them playing softly for their own pleasure in a corner of the room.

Jim doubles on baritone sax and plays it as well as he does soprano. His slow ballads on the big horn are especially moving. (Los Angeles, 1993)

Jim, a Canadian by way of Scotland, is one of my all-time favorite musicians. He gets a gorgeous sound from this little soprano sax, which he has owned since about 1950. (Odessa, 1989)

At the 1995 Odessa party, Jim and Dan Barrett, *right,* got together in one of those wonderful after-hours sessions where they play quietly in a corner of the hospitality room, accompanied by bass or guitar.

Bobby Gordon

Bobby creates on his clarinet the most beautiful plaintive sound I have ever heard. He is very shy and reserved, reflecting his playing. Bobby says what he has to say through his music. He plays exciting up-tempo clarinet and has a pleasant singing voice; but for a slow ballad, he's my man.

Bobby started out working and studying with the great clarinetist Joe Marsala. I first heard him when he was a member of Jim Cullum's band, based in San Antonio. After leaving Cullum, Bobby moved to New York and worked with Ed Polcer and the band at Condon's. He has a steady gig at Mulligan's in San Diego but also plays jazz parties in all parts of the world, either as a soloist or with Marty Grosz and the Orphan Newsboys.

One night years ago, I was listening to the World's Greatest Jazz Band at a New York club. Bobby showed up, and Yank Lawson invited him to sit in. Sol Yaged arrived, and Yank asked him and his clarinet to join the band. Bob Wilber, a member of the WGJB promptly picked up *his* clarinet.

Whereupon Yank announced that he would like Bud Freeman to put down his tenor sax and play clarinet. Bud, a giant on tenor, was not a talented clarinetist. Comparing the sound of the projected clarinet quartet with that of a flock of chickens, Yank told the crowd, "We will now hear sunrise on a guinea farm."

After leaving the Jim Cullum band, Bobby worked at Condon's in New York. This shot shows him with Chris Griffin, who played trumpet with Harry James and Ziggy Elman in the great Benny Goodman band of the '30s. That's Jack Lesberg on bass and Jimmy Andrews on piano. (New York, 1978)

Bobby played clarinet at all of Joe Boughton's jazz parties at a quaint old hotel in Conneaut Lake, Pennsylvania, during the '80s. (Conneaut Lake, 1988)

Bobby helped make Condon's my first stop every time Ann and I went to New York. Here he's
playing with Jack Lesberg and Pee Wee Erwin, *left and center.* (New York, 1978)

Urbie Green

Urbie is one of the master jazz trombonists. Primarily a big band player, he worked with Gene Krupa and Woody Herman in the late '40s and early '50s, and in the '60s he fronted the Tommy Dorsey Orchestra.

I first heard Urbie at the jazz weekend put on by Dick Gibson at Elitch Gardens in Denver in the summer of 1968. He was featured with only piano, bass, and drums (Dick Hyman, Jack Lesberg, and Mousie Alexander) and sounded wonderful. Urbie worked all the Gibson parties of the '70s, and also many other later parties.

In 1968, he recorded an album called *21 Trombones*. It featured twenty-one trombone players (of course), among them Will Bradley, J.J. Johnson, Lou McGarity, Buddy Morrow, Sonny Russo, Kai Winding, and Urbie himself, plus a rhythm section that included Bucky Pizzarelli, George Duvivier, and Bobby Rosengarden. It is one of the most striking albums I have ever heard. That same year, Urbie made another album with the same title. This one had twenty-five trombonists and a rhythm section including Dick Hyman, Bernie Leighton, Tony Mottola, Bob Haggart, and Grady Tate.

I heard Urbie at the 1996 party of the New Jersey Jazz Society at Waterloo Village. He again worked with just piano, bass, and drums (this time Derek Smith, Frank Tate, and Joe Ascione) and sounded just as great as he did twenty-eight years earlier in Denver.

During a tour with a great band led by Pee Wee Erwin, Urbie enjoyed a late supper in the living room of my friend Robert Nixon. The group also included Bob Wilber, Dave McKenna, Major Holley, and Bobby Rosengarden. (Pine Bluff, 1979)

Urbie is an unusually strong trombonist with great range. His high notes are especially beautiful. (Minneapolis, 1988)

To Al good luck Urbie Green

To Al Chuck Mann(?)

To Al Slam Stewart

To Al: Joe Wilder

At the 1972 Colorado Springs party, Urbie played a set with Slam Stewart and Joe Wilder, *center and right.*

Al Grey

Al, a marvelous trombonist, is one of the most exciting of the numerous musicians who became known while members of the Count Basie band. Like so many of the players profiled in this book, he developed his own sounds. Al creates one of his most unique effects by putting a small straight mute into the bell of his horn, and then a plunger mute or plumber's helper. Using these mutes, he brings tears to many eyes playing a ballad such as George Gershwin's "Summertime."

Al has an infectious laugh and keeps things hopping when he's on the stand. During one of his beautiful muted ballad solos one afternoon at the Odessa party, a three-year-old child in the front row turned to his father and asked loudly, "Daddy, what's he doing?" The youngster's question broke up Al as well as the audience. "I'm supposed to be a professional, and a kid steals my act," he told Ann and me.

A twelve-year-old boy who was studying trombone came to another Odessa party with his father. Al gave the boy a free lesson every afternoon at the party and continued to do so for the next several years.

Al and Buddy Tate, also a Basie veteran, worked up an act with local rhythm sections featuring "Jumpin' at the Woodside" and other Basie hits. They received standing ovations throughout the world. Al's luggage got lost before one concert, and the only thing available for him to wear was a tux about four sizes too large and a tiny bow tie. The sight of Al in this outlandish outfit made Buddy laugh so hard that he could hardly play.

Al, standing between Trummy Young and Marshall Royal, listens to Ruby Braff soloing at the 1978 Colorado Springs party. Al and Marshall, who played alto sax, spent years together in the Basie band.

I took this photo one afternoon while Al was playing a beautiful solo of "Summertime." A three-year-old boy sitting in the front row broke up Al and the audience when he turned to his father and asked loudly, "Daddy, what's he doing?" (Odessa, 1982)

Al, shown with fellow trombonist Bill Watrous, was one of Count Basie's top sidemen during the '50s and '60s. He has a distinctive style that is easily recognized, featuring a straight metal mute with a rubber plunger. (Colorado Springs, 1978)

Marty Grosz

Marty not only plays wonderful acoustic guitar, but for me his quick wit makes him the most entertaining jazz musician since the early 1970s. This guy keeps the audience laughing by saying whatever pops into his mind—about the audience itself, the place where he's playing, the musicians he's playing with, or anything else. Marty is a delightful singer, too.

I've always loved the sound of a quartet made up of cornet, clarinet, guitar, and bass. Marty's rhythm is infectious, and he fronts a swinging combo, the Orphan Newsboys, which also features Peter Ecklund, Bobby Gordon, and Greg Cohen. The blend of top jazz and unrestrained humor never fails to win wild applause.

Marty's father was George Grosz, a fine artist who did a lot of work for *Esquire* magazine. The family got out of Germany just in time before Hitler took over. Marty spent his early professional years playing in Chicago. Bob Wilber and Kenny Davern brought him aboard their newly formed Soprano Summit, and he was on his way.

Marty, Kenny, and Dick Wellstood played in Pine Bluff, and then went down to Jackson, Mississippi, for my friend Merrill Harris. The trio performed beautifully. The only trouble was that Marty's verbal meanderings had Dick and Kenny laughing so hard that they frequently had trouble playing. Marty also has a serious side and is a walking history of classic jazz.

Marty fronts the Orphan Newsboys, a combo with Greg Cohen, Peter Ecklund, and Bobby Gordon, *left to right*. This group played for the opening of the Arts and Science Center in Pine Bluff in 1994. (Los Angeles, 1993)

Marty and Joe Venuti, *left,* were in the lobby of the Broadmoor Hotel working out the next set when I asked them to play "Changes," and away they went. Joe had played this tune with Paul Whiteman in the '20s when Bix Beiderbecke was in the band. (Colorado Springs, 1977)

Hal Smith, *right,* a top drummer, often works jazz parties with Marty. I love the way Marty, after a jazz band has started a tune, spontaneously directs each musician to do certain things, in effect writing an arrangement while the tune is being played. (Pensacola, 1990)

Bobby Hackett

I first saw Bobby in 1952 at the Hickory House in New York. From my table just a couple of feet away, I noticed a little tin pie pan sitting upside down next to his right foot. Bobby set the tempo for each tune by tapping on the pan. His sidemen included Vic Dickenson on trombone and Gene Cedric, Fats Waller's clarinet player.

Bobby played guitar and then cornet in Glenn Miller's great band. His cornet solo on "String of Pearls" has perhaps been copied and heard more than any other solo in jazz history. When a band plays the Miller arrangement today, Bobby's solo is written out for the entire trumpet section.

Some of Bobby's most delightful music can be heard on the Chiaroscuro CDs recorded by his quintet at the Roosevelt Grill. He and Vic were backed by Dave McKenna, Jack Lesberg, and Cliff Leeman.

The music seems to flow effortlessly from Bobby's horn, and he can be recognized after just a few bars of a tune. Musicians whom I have talked to about Bobby agree to a man that he played almost perfectly.

Bobby's trumpet was in its case when I asked to take his picture. "Wait a minute," he said, pulling out the horn. He inserted the mouthpiece and *then* posed for me. A beautiful man and a beautiful player. (Vail, 1970)

Peanuts Hucko, *left,* and Benny Carter, *right,* watch Bobby and Vic Dickinson play one of their inimitable duets. Major Holley is on bass and Oliver Jackson on drums. Bobby and Vic worked together so frequently that their timing was absolutely perfect. (Colorado Springs, 1973)

Bobby and Vic Dickinson had tremendous mutual respect as musicians and great love for
each other as individuals. This photo shows the pleasure I got from their feelings. (Vail, 1970)

Bob Haggart

Bob did it all. He not only ranks among the greatest bass players of all time, but also is famous as a composer and arranger. Hag's compositions include such jazz standards as "What's New?", "South Rampart Street Parade," "My Inspiration," and the zany "Big Noise from Winnetka." His arrangements helped make the Bob Crosby orchestra a standout of the Big Band Era.

Hag was also an excellent artist. Four of his oil paintings hang in my home.

In the spring of 1968, Ann and I went to New Orleans for a jazz fest. We were having lunch at the Court of Two Sisters when Ann commented that the man and woman at the adjacent table were the handsomest couple she had ever seen. I recognized the man as Bob Haggart and rushed over and introduced myself. He was with his lovely wife, Windy. Her real name was Helen, but she picked up the nickname because she talked a lot. Everyone called her Windy, which she enjoyed. It didn't bother her a bit.

Bob told me that a great band would be playing at Elitch Gardens in Denver that summer. The musicians, called the Ten Greats of Jazz, were Yank Lawson, Billy Butterfield, Cutty Cutshall, Lou McGarity, Peanuts Hucko, Bud Freeman, Ralph Sutton, Clancy Hayes, Haggart, and Morey Feld. I went to Denver and was blown away by unquestionably the best jazz I had ever heard.

Bob and Windy were among our closest friends. Sadly, she died in 1993, and Bob passed away in 1998.

Hag abused alcohol in his younger days. He became and continues to be, even in death, a big help in my daily struggle not to drink. Bob was one of the finest men I have ever known, and my best buddy in the jazz world.

Bob and Jack Lesberg, *right,* two premier bass men, pose with Hag's famous bass. It belonged to Bob Casey when Casey was playing with Jimmie Noone in Chicago during the '30s. (Aspen, 1994)

Bob and drummer Ray Bauduc, *right,* delighted the crowd with "Big Noise from Winnetka" at the 1985 Mid-America Jazz Festival in St. Louis. They dreamed up the classic novelty tune on the spur of the moment in 1937 at the Blackhawk Restaurant in Chicago.

Of all the musicians I have met, I consider Bob my best friend. He provided invaluable assistance in helping me stop drinking. I will forever love him. (Conneaut Lake, 1992)

If you look closely, you can see the indentation on the tip of Bob's right index finger resulting from all those years of playing bass. Hag stood behind my eleven-year-old son, Al III, for this 1968 photo at Elitch Gardens in Denver.

Scott Hamilton

When Scott and his tenor sax appeared on the jazz scene in the early '70s, it seemed that Coleman Hawkins had come to life stronger and better than ever. Scott cannot read music, but his amazing ear enables him to play gorgeously in any musical setting. He plays the most modern numbers and also boots home the front line of a traditional jazz band. On the stand, in an effort to make his sax sound better or to find a perfect reed, Scott has the habit of disassembling the horn while another musician is soloing.

I especially enjoy the duo-tenor recordings that Scott and Flip Phillips have made. Their Concord CD called *A Sound Investment* was exactly that. Scott and Warren Vaché teamed up with Rosemary Clooney on some other wonderful albums. Scott has done a number of CDs, also on Concord, with a fine quintet featuring John Bunch (on whom there's a section in this book), Chris Flory, Phil Flanigan, and Chuck Riggs. Photos of Chris, Phil, and Chuck are on pages 86 and 87.

Milt Hinton tells the story of when Scott first played in New York and asked to sit in at Michael's Pub, where Milt was fronting a combo. Scott sounded great, and the boss told Milt to give him a week.

A few days later Scott brought in Chris, who played guitar so well that the boss told Milt to give him a week, too.

But when Scott brought in Phil, Milt said, "Now wait a minute!" He then called Ed Polcer at Condon's to see if there was a spot there for the young bassist.

Chuck played drums with Bob Wilber in my playroom one night and tried to persuade me to sell him the huge Chinese cymbal that I got from Cliff Leeman. Every time I see Chuck he asks me about "old China boy."

In 1981, Scott and Flip Phillips, *right,* posed with my wife, Ann, between sets of their twin tenor gig at the Blackstone Hotel in Chicago. A button came off Ann's dress. Scott took us to his very tidy room with all the Coleman Hawkins and Ben Webster tapes, got out his sewing kit, and refastened it.

Scott's beautiful fat and gutty tone can almost be heard in this photo. It is remarkable that a man who never learned to read music produces such an exciting sound on tenor sax. (Conneaut Lake, 1987)

Here's a shot of Scott and Flip Phillips, *left,* one of the top tenor sax teams I've ever heard, in action with Jake Hanna on drums.
Scott and Flip can take an old tune such as "Maria Elena" and turn it into a jazz classic. (Minneapolis, 1987)

Scott Hamilton's Sidemen

Chris Flory posed with Scott Hamilton, *right,* at the 1989 Mid-America Jazz Festival in St. Louis. This photo shows the great respect they have for each other.

Phil Flanigan is especially effective working in a small group or with just a piano player. Phil and John Bunch, also a member of Scott Hamilton's quintet, teamed up on a tasty CD called *Struttin'*. (Clearwater 1998)

Chuck Riggs, shown here with Bob Wilber, is a fine straight-ahead drummer who has worked with most of my favorite players. (St. Louis, 1984)

Jake Hanna

Jake played in the famous Woody Herman bands of the '60s. He has a wonderful sense of humor and shouts encouragement to his favorite soloists from behind the drums. Through the years, Jake has worked a lot with Ralph Sutton. When Ralph starts stretching out with some stomping stride piano, Jake yells, "Ralphie!"

I love Jake's cymbal work. His sock cymbals and two ride cymbals look like he's been using them for at least 100 years. He also has a large Chinese cymbal to his right that's suspended by paper clips from an old music stand. Jake knows just how to use these cymbals to make the players on the front line sound great.

Jake was especially pleased with a picture I took of him, and so I gave him the negative. He used the photo on a fine Concord album called *No Bass Hit* that he recorded with Scott Hamilton and Dave McKenna—just tenor sax, piano, and drums.

Jake's wife, Denisa, has made a name for herself as an expert bowmaker. I watched her working at the Odessa party one year as she fashioned a type of exotic black wood into a bass bow for Michael Moore.

Jake was probably yelling "Ralphie!" when I snapped Ralph Sutton, Milt Hinton, and him, *left to right,* at the 1976 Odessa party. The cymbal placement tells me that Jake was playing Cliff Leeman's drums. Ralph's comment about being my marriage counselor is explained in his vignette.

Jake is one of the top jazz drummers, and his quick sense of humor makes him a marvelous all-around entertainer as well. He often breaks up a jazz party audience and the band by commenting on one of the other musicians with a wisecrack—insulting or otherwise. (Indianapolis, 1995)

I love this shot of Jake playing a four-bar break on the out chorus of a swinging jazz tune. (Odessa, 1977)

Bob Havens

Bob played trombone with the Lawrence Welk orchestra for twenty-two years, and, Welk considered him the greatest jazz musician with whom he had ever worked. Welk and jazz usually don't appear together in the same sentence. Nevertheless, I regard Bob as the finest natural talent on classic jazz trombone of the period covered by this book.

Bob received thorough musical training, having learned violin (whose music is written in the treble clef) before taking up trombone (a bass clef instrument). He was heavily influenced by Jack Teagarden.

A quiet man, Bob keeps pretty much to himself. He has stayed in my playroom several times during gigs in Pine Bluff and makes cassette copies of my old recordings of Louis Armstrong and Teagarden playing together and of Bob Crosby's Bob Cats.

I am a self-taught terrible trombone player. Bob has a collection of brass mouthpieces for trombone, and so whenever I see an unusual one I get it and save it for him.

Bob comes about as close as anyone to duplicating the sound of Jack Teagarden's trombone. He holds the slide between his index and middle fingers, as Jack did. (Pine Bluff, 1995)

Bob played with Ray McKinley and Dick Cathcart, *left and center,* at the 1986 Conneaut Lake party. He and Dick worked together in the Lawrence Welk orchestra.

Jack Teagarden was the first trombonist to remove the bell from his horn and play into a glass. Bob is a master of this difficult trick, which requires changing all the positions on the slide and holding the glass under his chin. (St. Louis, 1997)

Chuck Hedges

Chuck was one of Wild Bill Davison's favorite clarinet players. He is popular at jazz parties throughout the world. Chuck usually brings his own microphone, explaining that it enables him to hear himself better.

One year at the Indianapolis party, Chuck's girlfriend put her soft contact lenses into a glass of water and he accidentally swallowed them. The poor girl stared myopically at Chuck during the whole weekend. He announced toward the end of the gig that he thought he had lost his in-sight.

When Chuck played with Wild Bill and the audience got a little restive late in the evening, Bill would tell him, "Go out there and get them." Chuck would call an up-tempo tune such as "After You've Gone" and bring the crowd to its feet.

At a jazz party in Memphis, Chuck worked with Wild Bill but teamed up for a set with Allan Vaché, who was then on clarinet with the Jim Cullum band. They knocked everyone out. Bill came on next and fussed about having to follow every clarinet player in the country. "Bill," Milt Hinton advised him, "just have Chuck play a ballad and you'll get the audience back." Chuck did just that.

Chuck uses a special microphone (shown here) that he takes to most of his gigs along with his clarinet. He says it helps him hear himself better while playing. (Indianapolis, 1990)

Chuck and Tom Saunders, *right,* have worked together for years at many jazz parties. They have developed a marvelous blend of sound, especially when Bill Allred joins them in the front line on trombone. (Atlanta, 1994)

At the 1982 Mid-America Jazz Festival in St. Louis, Chuck performed with, *left to right,* Milt Hinton, Barrett Deems (barely visible on drums), Wild Bill Davison, and Harry Graves.

Joel Helleny

Joel has an individual trombone style that is characterized by a rough, gutty tone. There's a lot of Vic Dickenson in his playing. One of the top trombonists on the East Coast, Joel grew up in Texas but talks like a Yankee. Maybe he's been in New York too long.

During the '90s, Joel started turning up at more and more jazz parties. I took my first pictures of him at an after-hours session at the Odessa party. When I next saw Joel at the New Jersey Jazz Festival in Waterloo Village and asked him to autograph the photos for me, he looked at them and asked, "Who's the ugly guy?"

On a CD that Kenny Davern made for Arbors, Joel and Dan Barrett team up for a trombone duet on "Sidewalks of New York." Floyd Levin describes their head arrangement in his liner notes: "Barrett leads with his emphatic 'ya-ya' tones swapping phrases with Helleny's sensuous growls." Joel and Dan recorded the duet on the first take. Kenny liked it so much that he made it the title track of the album—*East Side, West Side*—even though he himself didn't play on the tune.

The first time I asked Joel to autograph one of my photos, he wanted to know, "Who's the ugly guy?" He has asked the same question every time since. (Clearwater, 1996)

After playing a set with Joel, Jake Hanna ran up to me and said, "Quick, grab your camera." He had noticed the No Smoking badge on Joel's lapel and had to have a *corpus delicti* photo of the trombonist. (Hoboken, 1995)

At a performance for the New Jersey Jazz Society, Joel played in a great front line with Kenny Davern and Jon-Erik Kellso, *left and center*.
(Hoboken, 1995)

Eddie Higgins

Eddie was the house piano player in many Chicago jazz spots during the '50s and '60s. He started appearing on the rosters of various jazz parties in the '80s. Eddie has a quick wit and tells the audience a new story or two at every party.

Eddie always gets a laugh when he recalls the time he was in the Army and stationed in Central America. He entered an all-Army talent contest in an effort to escape from the heat of the Panama Canal region. Eddie went all the way to the finals in Fort Dix, New Jersey, where he lost to an accordion player who had packed the house with relatives.

In the contest, Eddie played "St. Louis Blues" as a boogie number at a bat-out-of-hell tempo. It remains one of his most popular specialties. The arrangement that he gives the drummer includes the following directive: "As fast as you can play on the last three choruses."

Eddie is one of the most underrated pianists on the jazz scene. He was the house piano player in the top Chicago clubs of the '50s and '60s, backing the headline artists who played there. (St. Louis, 1988)

A set at the 1986 Wilmington party featured Eddie and Derek Smith, *right.* Kenny Davern introduced them as "the Ferrante and Teicher of jazz." Boy, did they put on a show.

Eddie plays a sensational boogie version of "St. Louis Blues." He wrote a drum part that includes instructions to do the last three choruses "as fast as you can play." (Wilmington, 1987)

Milt Hinton

It's easy to understand why Milt is called The Judge. He picked up this nickname years ago because musicians have such tremendous respect and affection for him.

Milt played bass with Cab Calloway's band during its heyday of the 1930s and 1940s. Because of his exceptional ability to read anything put before him, as well as being a thrilling improviser, Milt probably has taken part in more jazz recordings than any other musician. Younger players are especially fond of him because he has helped so many of them early in their careers. Jay Leonhart and Brian Torff have written songs and poems about Milt.

During the years that Milt played the Odessa Jazz Party, he got several other musicians up in the morning to go with him to various schools and play for the kids. I went along many times, and the guys played as well for the children as for the paying audience. Milt displayed his great sense of humor one day when he and I were left with a three-year-old boy while waiting for the car that took us back to the hotel. Milt tried to entertain him, but the child began to cry. "Son," Milt told him, "I know you've seen sun tans before, but you must think this is ridiculous."

Milt's wife, Mona, is a fixture at virtually all the jazz parties where he plays. She almost always calls him Milton, not Milt. They have been together since 1939.

The Judge inspired me to create this book because he captured much of the Big Band Era with his camera. His two books of photos, *Bass Line* and *Over Time,* are a history of his life in jazz. David Berger and his wife, Holly Maxson, helped Milt with those books, and they gave me encouragement and advice in preparing *Jazz Party.*

Milt posed with Pee Wee Erwin, *center,* and me at the 1980 Odessa party. Milt and Pee Wee were very good friends and, with Bob Haggart, are among the musicians to whom I feel closest. The little half-moon scar above Pee Wee's upper lip resulted from more than sixty years of blowing a trumpet.

This is one of the few photos I have of Milt in a coat and tie. He was working with Dick Hyman's Perfect Jazz Repertory Quintet, and Dick asked all the musicians to wear band uniforms. (Conneaut Lake, 1984)

Milt and Mona, his wife, *left,* got together with Holly Maxson and David Berger at a concert sponsored by the New Jersey Jazz Society. David was a bass student of Milt's as a kid, and they became close friends. He and Holly, his wife, helped Milt with his two great books of jazz photos, and they encouraged me to prepare this book. (Hoboken, 1995)

Late one night during the 1984 Odessa party, Milt was flanked by Dan Barrett, *left,* and Harry Allen, *right.* This is my favorite kind of jazz: great musicians playing quietly after hours for themselves in a corner of the hospitality room.

Art Hodes

Art cut his teeth playing piano in Chicago joints, chiefly on the South Side, owned by gangsters of the '20s. He also became a widely read jazz historian.

During the '40s, Art produced a monthly magazine called *The Jazz Record,* which featured articles about jazz musicians and their world. Many of these articles appeared in *Selections from the Gutter,* a book by Art and Chadwick Hansen. The two men teamed up again on Art's candid biography, *Hot Man.*

Whenever Art toured in the Pine Bluff area, he played a gig for us, usually with three other Chicagoans—Franz Jackson on tenor sax, Jimmy Johnson on bass, and Hillard Brown on drums. Hillard belted out a tasty vocal on "Kansas City Blues." When Robert Nixon and I were in the audience, Hillard threw in his own words to the part about standing on 8th Street and Vine: "Al, when I saw you and Doc, I could hardly keep from crying."

Art was one of the great blues piano players. He helped jazz fans like me understand the music and worked throughout his life spreading the joy of this only true American art form. (Pine Bluff, 1980)

In 1981, Ann and I were in Chicago, and I hung out with Art every minute I could. We spent a day together in his home, and I had fun digging through old copies of *The Jazz Record* magazine, which Art published during the '40s.

To Al W — who made so much possible — Art Hodes — June 84 —

Art, together with Kenny Davern and Don DeMichael, *left a*nd *center,* played some dates in Arkansas in 1980, and I saw them off at the Little Rock airport. They billed themselves as the Hot Three, and they sure were.

Major Holley

Major, a big, friendly guy, loved life and people who appreciated his art. He combined the skills of a fine bass player and a delightful entertainer. Major adopted Slam Stewart's technique of comic humming-singing along with his bowed solos. However, Major vocalized in unison with his bowing, while Slam did so an octave higher. Major's ultradeep voice added to the hilarity of his performances. The two bassists made a marvelous LP together, with Dick Hyman on piano and organ and Oliver Jackson on drums.

Dick Gibson hired Major for one of his parties, but Mule (Major's nickname) did not show up. Soon after that, Dick ran into him pushing his bass in downtown New York and asked what had happened. Replied Major, "Man, wasn't I there?"

The last time I saw Major before his death, he was touring with Pee Wee Erwin. They played in Pine Bluff, and we all had dinner at the home of Janey and Robert Nixon. Major and Pee Wee spent the night with Ann and me. This was in the middle of the cotton season, and I had to get up early.

When I went into the kitchen the next morning, there was Major having a cup of coffee. Pee Wee had told him about my interest in Civil War relics, and Major wanted to see my collection before I left for work. This happy man was interested in everything.

Major was as good on tuba as on string bass. I snapped this photo while he was working in a band led by trumpeter Spanky Davis in Jimmy Ryan's club. (New York, 1973)

Oh, how I miss this big guy. I put Major in a class with Milt Hinton and George Duvivier when ranking musical talent supplemented by ultrafriendliness to jazz fans like me. (Minneapolis, 1988)

The major was one of the best natural entertainers I have ever heard. He became known for his comic humming-singing when bowing a bass solo. Major was nicknamed "Mule" because of his great stamina on his large, bulky instrument. (Minneapolis, 1988)

Eddie Hubble

Eddie is probably the most underrated trombone player profiled in this book. He performed at Dick Gibson's jazz parties during the '70s, and Pee Wee Erwin used him whenever he was available. Eddie was on hand at many of the Odessa parties and played in the World's Greatest Jazz Band and Jim Cullum's band. He is also an excellent baritone horn player.

Eddie's father, a staff trombonist for a Los Angeles radio station, started his son on the horn when the boy was seven years old. At fifteen, Eddie was playing in the Hollywood USO canteen band with Ken Murray's Blackouts. His family moved to Scarsdale, New York, in 1944, and Eddie played in a high school combo there with Bob Wilber and Dick Wellstood.

Before he was twenty, Eddie had worked in the bands of Buddy Rich, Alvino Rey, and Jess Stacy. He later hung out and played with the Condon gang. On the night that Eddie Condon's first club opened in December 1945, he used a fake ID card to get in and heard the first tune played, "September in the Rain."

Eddie lost a leg in an automobile accident in 1979 at the age of fifty but began playing again as soon as he could. Warren Vaché told me of driving to gigs with Eddie sitting beside him in the front seat, his artificial leg slung over his shoulder like a rifle.

This 1984 photo shows Eddie at Condon's with Red Balaban, *left*. He wrote on it, "Can't wait for Jazzie 60." At my 50th birthday party, Eddie had played in a band led by Pee Wee Erwin. Each musician, at Ann's request, wore a T-shirt with "Al White is a Jazzie 50" printed on it. At the right is Palu, who doubles as fry cook and trumpet player. He listened to Ed Polcer so much that he began to sound like him.

Trombone is Eddie's main instrument, but he plays baritone horn equally well. In a set at the 1974 Odessa party, he worked with Kai Winding, *left*, and that's Bobby Rosengarden behind him on drums. The "Doc" in Eddie's inscription is my close friend Robert Nixon.

Eddie plays a trombone with an oversized bell. He has filed all the regular braces off the bell so that it "rings" better. Here he's playing with, *left to right,* Jack Lesberg, Pee Wee Erwin, Johnny Best, and Bobby Rosengarden. (Odessa, 1974)

Peanuts Hucko

Peanuts started out playing tenor sax in Will Bradley's fine band that had Ray McKinley on drums. During World War II, he played sax with Glenn Miller's Army Air Force Band in England. He and Ray gigged around New York after the war, and at one session Peanuts picked up a clarinet. "What are you going to do with that?" Ray asked. Peanuts showed him.

He became a member of the Condon gang and was featured on many of Condon's great recordings. One of my favorite albums of all time is *Jazz Ultimate,* which Bobby Hackett and Jack Teagarden did for Capitol. On one track, Peanuts plays a tenor solo that shows off his versatility. He also played with Benny Goodman and Louis Armstrong's All Stars.

At a 1992 concert in Germany, Peanuts and his own all-star crew recorded an excellent CD called *Swing That Music* for Star Line. His sidemen included Randy Sandke, Johnny Varro, and Butch Miles. Peanuts even sang a lively "When You're Smiling" with Louise Tobin, his wife and former vocalist for Benny Goodman. At a jazz party in Los Angeles, Peanuts fronted a big band and Louise sang. They sounded great in both venues.

Peanuts is a master at exciting a crowd with up-tempo versions of such tunes as "Stealing Apples" and "The World Is Waiting for the Sunrise." His clarinet shines just as brilliantly on "Just a Closer Walk with Thee," "Memories of You," and other ballads. (Colorado Springs, 1973)

At the 1989 Odessa party, Peanuts and his wife, Louise Tobin, *left,* posed with George and Ruby Tyler. Louise sang with Benny Goodman, and she still performs with Peanuts. George was coproducer with Bill McPherson of the Blue Angel recordings.

Peanuts and Flip Phillips, *center right,* were standing together when I sneaked up to the bandstand to get a shot of Ralph Sutton at the piano. As I turned to leave, Flip yelled, "Al, shoot us!" Here's the result, with Milt Hinton, *left,* and Butch Miles, *right.* (Odessa, 1989)

Dick Hyman

Dick is a marvelous pianist, both as a soloist and with a band, and also ranks as a fine arranger and composer. I have seen him hold audiences spellbound playing solo as he performs classic standards that they have heard countless times. His fast, intricate runs rival those of Art Tatum. In fact, Danny Barker, the guitarist of the Cab Calloway band, told me years ago that Dick was one of Tatum's favorites among the crop of young players.

Before a gig, Dick plays complex finger exercises and scales, often while reading a book or newspaper. Like Milt Hinton, he has appeared on an astonishing number of jazz recordings. Dick has been the music director of a number of Woody Allen's movies; for years he had the same role on Arthur Godfrey's radio show, working with such jazz artists as Lou McGarity and Johnny Mince.

Dick is a master at arranging tasty programs. For several years, the New Jersey Jazz Society put on a piano spectacular in which six or seven world-class pianists played a three-hour set. Dick designated the order in which they appeared, and who would be teamed with whom to play duets or even three-piano sets.

He and his wife, Julia, spent the night in my playroom in Pine Bluff, surrounded by photos, recordings, and other jazz memorabilia. Dick called it a "little jazz heaven."

Dick was playing a nine-foot concert grand piano when I shot this photo at the recording session for the Arbors double-CD called *Something Old, Something New,* featuring Jerry Jerome. (Bradenton, Florida, 1996)

Despite a steady schedule of gigs, Dick plays finger exercises before almost every performance. I took this shot of him practicing at the Wilmington party in 1988. It's an unusual scene because Dick is playing with his legs crossed.

As he does on virtually all his recordings, Dick played a vital role in the band that made Jerry Jerome's *Something New* CD.
The group consisted of, *left to right,* Dick, Bucky Pizzarelli, Randy Sandke, Jerry, Joe Ascione, Bob Haggart, and George Masso.

Keith Ingham

Keith is an English piano player who has lived in the United States since 1978. Marty Grosz calls him a "tune sleuth" because he searches junk shops throughout the world for old sheet music. Keith has used the music to put together some great CDs for bands and singers, the latter including Suzannah McCorkle and Barbara Lea. He was Suzannah's accompanist and musical director for several years.

I met Keith when he was traveling with one of the later editions of the Lawson-Haggart Jazz Band. While playing in Pine Bluff, the band stayed with Robert and Jane Nixon and Ann and me. Keith bunked with the Nixons. Robert has a collection of jazz recordings and books dating from the '50s, and he was awakened at about 5 a.m. by Keith's playing an old LP.

Joe Boughton, who put on the jazz party at Conneaut Lake, Pennsylvania, had some of the musicians play for Saturday brunch. One Saturday morning, I ran into Keith on his way downstairs to play. He wore a terrible scowl after being in a jam session in the bar almost all night. I told him I had never taken a good picture of him at the keyboard because he always hugged the keys. I gave him a big smile and asked for one in return.

Before starting to play, Keith told the audience that he had gotten up feeling dreadful, which lasted until he saw me smile. Then he ripped off the guttiest version I've ever heard of "Atlanta Blues."

I took this shot of Keith after he had played piano nearly all night in the hotel bar. He said it cheered him to see my smiling face, and he dedicated "Atlanta Blues" to me. (Conneaut Lake, 1992)

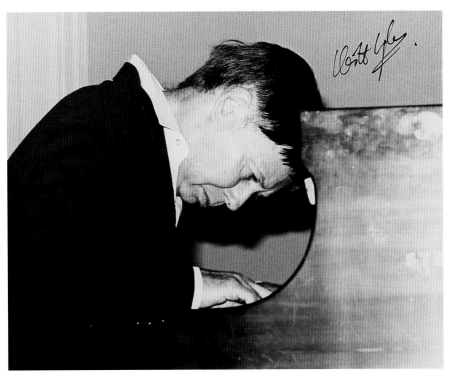

Keith played solo piano at one of the morning sessions of the 1992 Conneaut Lake party. He features such obscure tunes as "Mandy Lee Blues" and "Frisco Rider."

Under the watchful eye of the noted jazz photographer Duncan Schiedt, Keith played after hours in the hotel bar. Duncan, whose work has appeared in the top jazz publications, is also a good piano player. He knows thousands of tunes but could never stump Keith at any of these sessions. (Conneaut Lake, 1990)

Jerry Jerome

Jerry planned to be a physician, but his love for jazz and a lack of funds during the Great Depression pulled him out of medical school after two years. His tenor sax became a highlight of the bands of Benny Goodman and Artie Shaw.

I didn't hear Jerry in a live performance until Bob Haggart's 80th birthday party at the 1994 March of Jazz put on by Mat and Rachel Domber of Arbors Records. Although he was born two years before Bob, Jerry's enthusiasm belies his age. When Hag was introduced at the birthday party, Jerry grabbed his horn and blew the most raucous chorus imaginable of "The Old Gray Mare She Ain't What She Used to Be."

Jerry tells some great stories about his days with the Goodman band. During an engagement at the Paramount Theater in New York, he and Toots Mondello went to a novelty shop and bought some straws that contained little parachutes. When someone blew through the straws, the parachutes popped out and floated down. On the next set, while Benny was wailing away on "One O'Clock Jump" in front of the band, Jerry and Toots blew their tiny parachutes out on the stage behind him. The audience erupted in laughter, but Benny couldn't figure out what was going on. He finally turned to the band and asked, "Is my fly open?"

Jerry uses both words and music in reminiscing about his long and colorful career on *Something Old, Something New,* an Arbors double-CD. It includes a fascinating potpourri of recordings dating from 1939 to 1996, with Jerry's spoken narration.

Jerry and Bob Haggart, *right,* posed at the recording of the "new" part of Jerry's *Something Old, Something New* double-CD following the 1996 Clearwater party. These two jazz veterans did a lot of studio work together in the '40s and '50s.

I took this picture of Jerry at Bob Haggart's 80th birthday party. When Hag was introduced, Jerry grabbed his tenor sax and blew a wild chorus of "The Old Gray Mare She Ain't What She Used to Be." (St. Petersburg, 1994)

During this set at the 1996 March of Jazz, Jerry teamed with Rick Fay, *right*. Someone knocked Jerry's sax off the stand and it wouldn't make a sound. Jerry rushed his horn to the musicians' warm-up room because he knew Flip Phillips was there. Flip stuck a piece of cork into the sax and it sounded fine. (Clearwater, 1996)

Gus Johnson

Gus was my ribbon cane syrup pal. He loved this high-quality syrup, which is made from pure ribbon cane sugar stalks. Gus and Ralph Sutton were, as Al Grey remarked, as close as peas in a pod. The two friends played several gigs for us in Pine Bluff, and Gus always asked my son to get him six cans of ribbon cane syrup. Gus put each can in cotton wrapping paper and tied them together into a makeshift suitcase to take home on the plane.

Everyone who knew Gus was terribly saddened when Alzheimer's disease forced him to retire in 1990 at the age of seventy-seven. His condition became so bad that he had to be restrained in an institution.

Before succeeding Morey Feld as the drummer of the World's Greatest Jazz Band, Gus played with Count Basie and accompanied Ella Fitzgerald. He had the prettiest brush stroke and liked to release the snares on his snare drum while keeping the sound clear and in exactly the right spot.

Gus was a complete musician. If someone in the audience requested a tune that Gus knew but that was unfamiliar to any of the musicians, he quickly wrote it down on any available piece of paper. He composed a lovely ballad called "Under the Moonlight Starlight Blue" for the WGJB.

Gus and Milt Hinton had a routine in which they traded fours, twos, and finally just one bar at the end of an up-tempo tune. They always brought down the house.

This is my favorite photo of my old pal, Gus. I had sneaked around the side of the bandstand and yelled, "Hey, Gus!" Bob Haggart is on bass. (Indianapolis, 1988)

Gus took over my drums for a 1979 gig at the Pine Bluff Country Club with Kenny Davern and Ralph Sutton. Ralph, *left*, was joking with Kenny as they played.

Gus was a fine singer, especially on "Sweet Lorraine." He did a vocal at the Colorado Springs party in 1976, with Zoot Sims sitting in for him on drums. The other musicians were, *left to right,* Milt Hinton, Clark Terry, Frank Rosolino, and Benny Carter.

Max Kaminsky

Little Maxie's career began in the '20s when he was a kid trumpet player out of Boston. His life changed completely and forever after he went to Chicago and heard Bix Beiderbecke. Max wound up playing the jazz trumpet parts in the Tommy Dorsey band of the late '30s and then became a member of the Condon gang in New York. He also worked in Jimmy Ryan's club there.

Max was fronting a band in New Orleans in 1968 when I first met Bob Haggart. Hag played bass in the group and his son, Bob, Jr., was on drums. Max told me he had paid Pee Wee Russell before the band started to play and then caught the great clarinetist sneaking out the back door just as they were to go on. Maxie threatened to smack Pee Wee with his trumpet if he didn't stick around for the gig.

Another time, Max roomed with Eddie Condon while on the road. He remembered that Eddie got loaded every night and wanted to talk for hours in their room after they finished playing. Max got fed up with this routine one night and slugged Eddie on the chin, putting him out like a light. He was sure Eddie was too drunk to remember being socked, but the first thing his roommate said the next morning was, "Maxie, that was not a nice thing to do."

Ann and I went to Jimmy Ryan's one night to hear Max, and he showed me an album he had just made. I felt very proud to see one of my pictures on the cover. Max told his story in an excellent autobiography, *My Life in Jazz*, written with V.E. Hughes.

In 1978, Max played with Sal Pace, *left,* at Jimmy Ryan's in New York. I had the pleasure of buying Maxie's new album from him there and finding one of my photos on the cover.

Max told me a lot of stories from the Big Band days during a 1974 gig with Orange Kellen and Father Al Lewis, *both at left,* in Kerrville, Texas.

Max did a vocal while playing with Jim Cullum's Happy Jazz Band at the Landing in San Antonio in 1974. The others in the group were, *left to right,* Kevin Hess, Jim, Buddy Apfel, and Cliff Gillette.

Jon-Erik Kellso

To my ears, Jon-Erik is the answer of the '90s to Bobby Hackett and Ruby Braff, though Ruby still plays beautifully. This fine young cornetist was born in 1964, took up the trumpet at the age of ten, and has been playing gigs since he was fifteen.

Jon captures what Dick Wellstood called the grease and funk with which jazz should be played, keeping it pretty and clean at the same time. At the Conneaut Lake party in 1997, he impressed me with his ability to read arrangements that Dan Barrett had just written, and in the next set improvise with Marty Grosz. Jon has performed with other youthful East Coast musicians, such as Harry Allen, Scott Robinson, and Joe Ascione. He has made CDs for Arbors as both leader and sideman.

Jon plays an unusual cornet made by Bob DeNicola, the brother of drummer Tony DeNicola. It is called a puje trumpet and looks like an old shepherd's crook cornet but is more compact, and the bell angles to the left of the tubing. The tuning slide of the horn is in the mouthpiece, like that of a flugelhorn. Jon loves his puje trumpet and sounds wonderful on it.

Jon-Erik played at the 1994 Conneaut Lake party, where I told him the story of Dick Wellstood's proclaiming that good jazz needs a little grease and funk. Replied Jon, "Grease and funk are my middle name."

The audience at the 1997 party in Chautauqua, New York, heard Jon play his puje trumpet, *above*. He gets a lovely sound from the unusual horn.

This marvelous front line played at the Conneaut Lake party in 1994.
Jon was flanked by Bobby Gordon, *left,* and Bob Havens, *right.*

Rebecca Kilgore

Most jazz musicians and fans aren't too keen on female singers. A notable exception was Lee Wiley, who joined the Condon gang in the late '30s. Becky sings a lot like Lee did, without fooling around with the melody. A beautiful straight melody flows out when she sings.

Becky settled in Portland, Oregon, in 1979 and joined a local swing combo, Wholly Cats, as guitarist and vocalist. She then formed her own group, the Rebecca Kilgore Quintet.

In 1992, Dave Frishberg was asked to engage a singer for his solo piano gig at Portland's Heathman Hotel. He hired Becky, who quit her daytime job as a computer programmer and became a full-time vocalist. She performs not only with Dave, but also with her quintet, a country band called Beck-a-roo, and the Woody Hite Big Band.

Dan Barrett fronted a combo including Dave and Bucky Pizzarelli that backed Becky on her first CD, *I Saw Stars.* She also teamed up with Dave on such CDs as *Not a Care in the World* and *Looking at You.* Bucky declared that Benny Goodman would hire Becky if he were leading a band today.

Open and outgoing, Becky considers herself shy. She is refreshingly honest, with no pretense about her.

Rebecca is one of the two jazz singers who are profiled in this book. The other is Maxine Sullivan. Becky has the same natural, effortless delivery that featured Maxine's singing, and it knocked me out the first time I heard her. She also plays guitar and leads the Rebecca Kilgore Quintet. (Clearwater, 1997)

Becky has worked for years in a nightclub in Portland, Oregon, with Dave Frishberg, *left,* a fine piano player and composer. They have worked out many great arrangements and sound terrific together. (Clearwater, 1996)

At the 1995 Kingsport party, Becky sang a set accompanied by a band that included Ken Peplowski, *left,* and Eddie Erickson, *right.* She did several tunes from her Arbors album *I Saw Stars,* using some of the musicians from that recording.

Al Klink

Al replaced Bud Freeman on tenor sax in the World's Greatest Jazz Band. We met when the band played a college date in Cleveland, Mississippi. I reminded Al of one of the most famous Glenn Miller records, "In the Mood," on which he and Tex Beneke split the tenor solo. "I will never live that down," Al told me. Most musicians I have talked to agree that Al was a better jazz musician than Tex, but Tex was much better known because Glenn featured him as a vocalist.

Al also played with Benny Goodman and Tommy Dorsey and had a long career as a studio and club musician in New York. He later played at many jazz parties.

Wherever Al performed, he always practiced for a couple of hours before going on the stand. His dutiful preparation reminded me of Pee Wee Erwin, who put a mute in his trumpet and blew long tones by the hour prior to a performance. This procedure of Al's and Pee Wee's seemed to be a hallmark of many great musicians.

Al, seen here with Cliff Leeman, *left,* and Yank Lawson, *right,* was the tenor sax player with Tex Beneke for the famous four-bar exchange on Glenn Miller's "In the Mood." The general public never fully appreciated this fine musician. (Jackson, Mississippi, 1977)

When I went to the motel to pick up the WGJB for its 1974 Pine Bluff concert, Al was in his room blowing his sax as hard as he could. This photo features him during a solo, between Bob Wilber and Bob Haggart.

Shortly after Al replaced Bud Freeman in the World's Greatest Jazz Band in 1974, the group played a concert in Pine Bluff. The band also included Bob Wilber, *left,* and Bob Haggart and Yank Lawson.

Yank Lawson

Yank blew powerful lead trumpet and was a thoughtful, caring man. He was especially nice to my children.

I doubt if Yank let life trouble him in any way. One night I got extremely upset with him (I've forgotten why) during a gig in Pine Bluff. He gave me a big, sweaty hug in front of the audience and announced loudly, "Al thinks I don't like him. I love him." Another time, several musicians were talking about a colleague who had a reputation of being rather contentious. Said Yank, "I've never had a bit of trouble with him."

Ann and I and our kids took a trip up the East Coast and spent an evening with Yank and his wife, Harriet, at their home in Kennebunkport, Maine. Harriet fixed a delicious supper topped off by strawberry shortcake. Several times Ann looked like she would die when Yank took a bite of the shortcake and gave the next one to his huge black Labrador retriever.

Yank was a large man and became famous when he blew lead trumpet with the Bob Crosby band. He had the greatest capacity for vodka I have ever seen but played beautifully regardless. Yank stopped drinking several years before his death and kept blowing until the end.

Two small sidelights: Ann and Yank both were born on May 3, and Harriet and Yank shared November 18 as their wedding day with Ann and me.

Yank kept his distinctive trumpet sound until he died in 1995. He was a true free spirit, always playing his way no matter in what band—Bob Crosby, Tommy Dorsey, Benny Goodman—or at what jazz party he was performing. (Los Angeles, 1991)

I snapped Yank with Norma Teagarden, Jack's sister, at the 1986 Indianapolis party. Norma was an excellent pianist, and she and Yank had known each other for years; but they seldom had a chance to play together.

Yank posed with my seven-year-old daughter, Allyson, in Denver shortly after I met him at Elitch Gardens in 1968. As a little girl, Allyson would listen to my records and announce, "Yank Lawson is my favorite."

Cliff Leeman

Cliff traded two cymbals and a drumhead to me for an antique gun. My drums were thus enhanced by a huge Chinese cymbal that he used on the eight-bar intro to Artie Shaw's "Back Bay Shuffle." I also acquired Cliff's favorite ride cymbal, which got cracked when it was knocked off the stand at Condon's. I still use those cymbals. In addition, Cliff tossed in the bass drumhead that he used while with Woody Herman's band. On it an artist had painted the names of all of Woody's hits up until that time.

One of my favorite Condon LPs is *Jam Session Coast to Coast.* During "Ol' Miss," the rousing stem-winder, Cliff yells, "Hey, George!" George Wettling had failed to come in on the proper beat while they were trading four-bar drum breaks.

In 1977, Ann and I spent a few days with Cliff and his wife, Rene, at their home in New York. I had a lot of fun digging through his memorabilia and pictures dating back to the days with Shaw.

The Leemans drove us to Waterloo Village for the annual bash of the New Jersey Jazz Society. Cliff was rather fussy about other people touching his drums or having anything at all to do with them. As we neared the gate, he told Rene, who was driving, "Let me handle this." The guard saw the drums in the back seat and pointed the way to the music tent. Rene said thanks and drove in. "Goddammit, Rene, I wanted to do that!" Cliff bellowed.

Cliff was not flashy. But to me, he was one of the best and most exciting drummers.

Cliff was the last of the great time keepers. Pee Wee Erwin called him the finest rhythm drummer of them all. I thought this photo was one of my best of Cliff, but his inscription shows he disagreed. (Colorado Springs, 1978)

Cliff played my drums at a 1979 gig in Pine Bluff. He scratched out the "Ludwig" logo on the bass drum and wrote in "Slingerland," the name of the drum company whose products he endorsed.

AL
&
ANN

NOT OFTEN I DOUBLE DATE
BUT WHEN I DO
WHEE -SKIDDOO
x x x α

love
Rene

In 1977, Ann and I went to Condon's with Cliff and Rene Leeman while visiting the Leemans at their home. Cliff mugged between Rene, *left*, and Ann. On the stand in the background you can see, *left to right*, Marquis Foster, Red Balaban, Vic Dickenson, Ed Polcer, and Sam Margolis.

Jay Leonhart

Jay is popular at jazz parties as both a bass player and as a vocalist who delights audiences with witty songs that he writes himself. He became known as a composer-singer after gaining a reputation as a fine bassist. For a while he hoped that his success as a singer of funny songs wouldn't hurt his standing as a musician. Jay performs his tunes with a combo or accompanying himself on bass.

I met Jay in 1995 when I went to the jazz party put on by the New Jersey Jazz Society at Waterloo Village. Ed Polcer and his wife, Judy, took me to a club named Zinno's for dinner and to hear the tasty combo called New York Swing, which highlights the talents of John Bunch, Bucky Pizzarelli, and Jay. They have an arrangement of "Azure-Te" ("Paris Blues") on which Jay sounds especially great. The combo has made several CDs, and Jay also records under his own name.

Jay's love for Milt Hinton impresses me deeply. He wrote a tune that he sang at the famous bassist's 80th birthday celebration in 1990. The song tells how Milt befriended Jay when the young and unknown musician moved to New York. Jay sings about how "my telephone began to ring with gigs for me" after Milt spread the word about the talented new bass player in town.

I snapped this shot just after Jay, *right,* John Bunch, *left,* and Bucky Pizzarelli had finished a set. Ralph Sutton and Milt Hinton, *second and third from left,* made a special effort to hear them.

Jay is one of the top New York bass players and also ranks as a top entertainer who sings his own witty songs. These three photos were taken at a 1995 concert in Hoboken given by the New Jersey Jazz Society.

Jay and his wife, Donna, *left,* posed with Milt and Mona Hinton between sets. Just after Jay moved to New York in 1961, Milt opened the way to many gigs for the young bassist. Jay paid tribute to Milt in a lovely song about their early friendship.

Jack Lesberg

Jack wore two musical hats for a number of years. He played bass in the New York Philharmonic Orchestra under Leonard Bernstein and, as soon as the concert ended, rushed down to Eddie Condon's and played jazz the rest of the night.

Earlier in his career, in 1942, Jack played in the band at the Coconut Grove in Boston. He suffered serious injuries when a terrible fire destroyed the nightclub, though luckily he wasn't burned externally. The heat of the acrid smoke singed Jack's lungs, and then he got pneumonia. He spent about a month in the hospital and was on the critical list for part of that time.

At the suggestion of Ralph Sutton, Dick Gibson called Jack to help organize his first jazz party. Dick didn't know any musicians personally then, but Jack knew them all and made the contacts. He has been the music director of many parties through the years, working out the personnel and format of each set. The music director decides who plays with whom, when, and for how long; who leads the set; and who has a solo feature.

Jack was a charter member of the old Condon gang and played on many of the group's famous records. I'm especially fond of two of his recordings: one on Chaz Jazz of live performances by Jack and Ralph at Hanratty's in New York, and a Chiaroscuro CD of acoustic bass and guitar by Jack and Howard Alden. Appropriately, the latter is called *No Amps Allowed*.

One night while Jack was playing at Condon's, he joined Clive Acker and my wife, Ann, at our table. Clive produced the fine Jump record label during the early '40s (New York, 1978)

Jack helped Dick Gibson put his first jazz party together. This legendary bass player knows which musical personalities fit together best, and he has served as music director for many parties through the years. (Odessa, 1982)

Getting together for an after-hours session at the 1993 Odessa party were, *left to right,* Bucky Pizzarelli, Jack Lesberg, George Masso, Joe Ascione, and Milt Hinton. Joe used his brushes on a package of photos I had given him. I wasn't the only one taking pictures. Milt had his camera ready, too.

George Masso

Of all the people I have known in the music business—or any other business—George is one of the nicest and kindest. If he spots me while warming up at a jazz party, he points his trombone at me and plays the first few bars of "Arkansas Traveler."

Both of George's parents were professional musicians. His father was a bandleader who played trumpet, and his mother played piano in silent movies and a variety of other settings. George became Jimmy Dorsey's lead trombonist in 1948 but entered academia a couple of years later. After earning bachelor's and master's degrees in music education, he taught in high school and at the University of Connecticut. In 1973, Bobby Hackett, a friend of his father's, persuaded George to return to the life of a free-lance jazz musician.

Years ago, George composed several lovely solo pieces with piano accompaniment for his wife, Louise, and their four children. "Suite for Louise" was written for trombone, tuba, and French horn. George wrote four pieces for trumpet: "Song for David," "Marjorie's Holiday," "Dance for Lisa," and "Paula Jeanne Polka."

At the Odessa party one year, George, Robert Nixon, and I were listening to the music together. I spilled my coffee on Robert, and five minutes later I dumped my Coke into his lap. Whereupon, Robert told George and me about an incident that occurred when he was a young Navy physician. Robert's corpsman had gone to the captain's house to help with some painting. When the corpsman returned, he was laughing so hard that he had trouble telling how the captain's son stepped into the paint bucket. The captain yelled at his son, "Willie, you are a clubfooted cocksucker!"

That's why George always greets me with, "How's your foot, Al?"

George, in addition to being a master trombone player, is one of the most kindhearted people I have ever known. He started out with Jimmy Dorsey, taught music at the high school and university levels, and then became a jazz musician again. (Pensacola, 1990)

I love this shot of three of my favorite trombonists. George found himself between Trummy Young, *left,* and Vic Dickenson, *right,* at the 1976 Colorado Springs party. Vic looks like he's trying to guess what Trummy and George are going to do next.

George, *right,* and Dan Barrett, *left,* posed with me at the 1994 March of Jazz. They do a beautiful version of "Get Out and Get Under the Moon," which Cutty Cutshall and Lou McGarity used to feature. George and Dan play the tune on their Arbors CD, *Let's Be Buddies.* (St. Petersburg, 1994)

Jimmie Maxwell

Jimmie, a graduate of the Big Band Era, was featured on trumpet by Benny Goodman in the '30s. I met him when he worked the Odessa Jazz Party of 1982. Chatting with the audience before playing a solo on Louis Armstrong's "West End Blues," Jimmie recalled a story about the famous original 1928 recording of the tune.

When Earl Hines heard the playback of Louis' introduction, said Jimmie, he advised Louis, "Pops, you better keep that one because neither you nor anyone else is going to play it better." Jimmie then told the Odessa crowd, "Now that I am properly nervous, I will try it." Did he ever!

During the '80s, Jimmie sometimes played at Eddie Condon's club. Once I saw him in a big band led by Bobby Rosengarden in the Rainbow Room at Rockefeller Center. Chatting with me between sets, Jimmie verified Lou McGarity's account of being fired by the World's Greatest Jazz Band because of his drinking. Lou moved in with Jimmie until he got back on his feet.

Jimmie was badly injured in an automobile accident one night while driving home from the Rainbow Room. He did not play again but was able to teach.

Jimmie played trumpet in the front line at Condon's with Bob Sparkman and Ed Polcer, *center and right,* in 1977. Benny Goodman featured Jimmie, whose style is reminiscent of Louis Armstrong's.

Jimmie, with Jake Hanna on drums, was playing the famous cadenza from the Louis Armstrong recording of "West End Blues" when I took this shot. (Odessa, 1982)

In 1982, Jimmie was in Bobby Rosengarden's band in the Rainbow Room in New York. During a break, I stepped up into the trumpet section and asked him to sign some pictures. My son, Al III, grabbed the camera and snapped Jimmie, *right,* and me.

Lou McGarity

While growing up, I rated Lou my favorite trombone player except for Jack Teagarden. I loved his work with Benny Goodman's band during the early '40s. Lou said Goodman auditioned about ten trombonists while forming that great band. After all of them had played, Benny asked Lou whom he liked best. Lou said Cutty Cutshall. Then Benny asked Cutty for his choice, and he named Lou. As a result, Goodman hired what I consider the best trombone duo ever.

Lou and Cutty teamed up on "Get Out and Get Under the Moon," and their performance still stands as my favorite trombone duet. Dan Barrett and George Masso always receive an ovation when they get together on the tune at jazz parties.

I met Lou at Elitch Gardens in Denver in 1968 when he was playing with the Ten Greats of Jazz, who became the World's Greatest Jazz Band. He was a kind, soft-spoken man. In 1970, Lou played at Dick Gibson's party in Vail, Colorado, and saw that I was drinking heavily. He told me that one night after giving up alcohol, he had a little wine with dinner and soon was again going through two quarts of vodka a day. The WGJB fired Lou because of his drinking.

That was probably the first time I realized that I had to do something about my booze problem. However, I did not stop drinking until after I met Pee Wee Erwin in the fall of 1971 at another Gibson party. Pee Wee also helped me, made me look at myself, and in March 1972 I finally quit. I've been dry ever since.

My friend Robert Nixon snapped this photo of Lou and me. I had been drunk the night before and ripped the seat of the only pants I had with me, so I had to keep my coat on for the rest of the party. This was the day that Lou talked to me about his own drinking and planted the seed that saved my life. (Vail, 1970)

Lou, an accomplished violinist as well as a great trombone player, is shown here with Joe Venuti, one of the most famous jazz violin players of all time. Lou was featured playing violin on "Tennessee Waltz," a 1953 recording by the Lawson-Haggart Jazz Band. (Vail, 1970)

To me, there has never been a trombone team like Lou and Cutty Cutshall, *right*. Their on-the-spot arrangement of "Get Out and Get Under the Moon" is played at every jazz party that features a trombone duet by such later greats as Dan Barrett and George Masso. (Denver, 1968)

Dave McKenna

Dave, like Ralph Sutton, is a wonderfully unique piano player. Dave's a big man, and it's amazing how his huge fingers put away those fast Art Tatum-like runs without missing a note. He plays a lot of stride and creates a sound that to me is remarkably like that of a guitar. I've never heard any other pianist produce that sound.

John Sheridan admires Dave for his quick thinking as well as his keyboard artistry. At the Pianorama of the New Jersey Jazz Society, Dave and John were chatting about the weather. A fan asked Dave what he planned to play during his solo segment. Dave said he hadn't decided. He started playing a few minutes later, and John recalls that his tunes included "Rain," "Isn't This a Lovely Day To Be Caught in the Rain," "On the Sunny Side of the Street," "Come Rain or Come Shine," and "When the Sun Comes Out."

The two pianists got together again just before Dave's solo set at the Conneaut Lake party. John remembers that they talked about the brightness of the moon. Sure enough, Dave played "Moon Over Miami," "Oh! You Crazy Moon," "What a Little Moonlight Can Do," "The Moon Got in My Eyes," "Paper Moon," "There Ought To Be a Moonlight Saving Time," and many other moon tunes.

Dave's wife, Frankie, has been a great help to him through the years, as Ann has been for me. He autographed a photo I had taken of him and wrote, "No more booze blues for you and me."

Dave is a shy, quiet man. After he played a concert in Pine Bluff, several people told me, "All he did was play the piano." I could have bitten a rock in half.

This photo catches Dave's remarkable reach of well over an octave on the piano. The little finger of his right hand is perpendicular to the keyboard. Dave's playing has a unique guitarlike sound to me. (Conneaut Lake, 1985)

Dave teamed up with Ralph Sutton, *left,* at the 1983 Odessa party. Many two-piano sets by these fabulous pianists get a noisier standing ovation than the finest full jazz band.

A band composed of, *left to right,* Bucky Pizzarelli, Buddy Tate, Dave McKenna, Milt Hinton, and Mousey Alexander played for schoolchildren during the Odessa party of 1975. The kids loved the music even though Dave's piano was a whole step out of tune and the sock cymbal on the drums was smashed flat.

Ray McKinley

Ray was extremely modest about his ability as a drummer. "I was never a Buddy Rich," he told me. "I just tried to keep time and entertain the audience." Ray did both superbly.

As a kid in the late '30s, I collected all the wonderful recordings of the band that Ray co-led with the great trombonist Will Bradley. In addition to his role as drummer, Ray won fame as a singer and composer. He wrote and did the vocal on one of the band's biggest hits, "Beat Me, Daddy, Eight to the Bar." Ray became the drummer in the Army band of Glenn Miller and took over its leadership after Miller was killed. Following the war, he led a fine band that featured the arrangements of Eddie Sauter.

Like many other top jazz artists, Ray worked as a studio musician during the '50s and '60s. I first met him when I was in the Army during the Korean War and heard him play weekend gigs at the Stuyvesant Casino in New York. He treated me and other jazz fans very kindly. Later, at jazz parties, he loved to talk about the great players with whom he had worked through the years, including Bob Haggart, Yank Lawson, and Bud Freeman. Born in Fort Worth, Ray never lost his Texas drawl.

Ray, a marvelous entertainer, did the vocal on "Beat Me, Daddy, Eight to the Bar," his own composition and one of the Will Bradley band's most famous hits. He also played drums in the Dorsey Brothers band until Jimmy and Tommy had a big fight and split. Ray went with Jimmy. (Conneaut Lake, 1984)

At the 1984 Conneaut Lake party, Ray teamed up with Bob Haggart, *right,* on Bob's "Big Noise from Winnetka." Ray was present in a New York hotel room when George Van Eps gave Bob his first music lesson—on guitar.

Here's another shot of Ray and Bob at Conneaut Lake in 1984. Ray was born in 1910 and Hag in 1914, and it was great fun to watch these two jazz masters play with the enthusiasm of much younger musicians.

Jay McShann

Jay, a wonderful jazz pianist and incomparable blues singer, is a self-taught musician. His sister used up all the money that the family had available for piano lessons. Jay's natural talent enabled him to learn everything he needed to know by hanging out in the hotbed of jazz in Kansas City during the '30s.

Jay is popularly known by his nickname, Hootie. When he began playing professionally with a band in Tulsa, he couldn't read a note of music. He fooled the leader, Al Dennie, for several months until one night when Al called a tune that started with a written piano solo. The other men in the band liked Jay's playing so much that they taught him to read music.

During the '30s, Jay led a big band in Kansas City that was the first to feature Charlie Parker, the alto sax great. He played many of the early Dick Gibson parties that I attended, and a number of other jazz parties through the years as well.

Jay and Ralph Sutton have a marvelous two-piano act that is billed as The Last of the Whorehouse Piano Players. They have made some excellent recordings and have played to sellout audiences throughout the world.

One of Jay's biggest fans is the English piano player Derek Smith, *left,* who posed with Jay and Bob Haggart, *right,* at the Mid-America Jazz Festival. Derek can be seen watching Jay's playing closely at every party where both perform. (St. Louis, 1995)

In addition to being a great jazz pianist, Jay is a matchless blues singer. Like Count Basie, he brought a fine band from Kansas City to New York in the late '30s. (Little Rock, 1984)

Neither Jay nor Ralph Sutton, *right,* has ever played piano in a whorehouse. That fact has not detracted from their great popularity as a team billed as The Last of the Whorehouse Piano Players. (St. Louis, 1984)

Butch Miles

Butch is a remarkable drummer who has done it all—from being featured in one of Count Basie's later bands to working in the pit bands of Broadway shows. He also has another string in his bow because he's a very entertaining singer. Butch does an amusing blues routine with a band, bringing in the names of other members of the group and even of people in the audience.

Early in his career, Butch played drums with Basie, which provided a fine training ground for him. I first heard him in 1972 with Mel Tormé at the Disney Park in Orlando, Florida. Mel played drums in his act, but Butch was featured. Butch has performed in all the top night spots in New York and on gigs throughout the world.

A pleasant, outgoing musician, Butch started playing jazz parties in the '70s. Audiences consider themselves lucky if the program teams him in a duet with Joe Ascione, Louie Bellson, or some other top drummer. After losing his wife, Lauri, in 1997, he played fewer parties because he was spending so much time on the road with the Basie band.

Butch gained fame while playing drums for Count Basie from 1975 to 1979. His work is always exciting and tasty, and Butch's outgoing personality enhances his stage presence greatly. (Indianapolis, 1990)

In addition to being one of the finest jazz drummers, Butch is an excellent blues singer. This photo caught him belting out one of his clever blues specialties in which he includes not only other band members, but also folks in the audience. (Odessa, 1985)

Butch obviously enjoyed himself when he joined Bob Haggart, *right,* at the 1994 Indianapolis party in performing Hag's intrepid "Big Noise from Winnetka." Yank Lawson, *left,* had a good time listening.

Eddie Miller

In the late '20s, during Eddie's early days as a musician, he was playing clarinet in a New Orleans club when Leon Roppolo came in. Roppolo had been the clarinetist in the New Orleans Rhythm Kings in Chicago but returned to New Orleans following a mental breakdown. When Eddie saw him enter the club, he tried to play as loud and fast as possible. Leon came up after the set and urged him to play fewer notes and try to make them all count. Eddie, who won fame on tenor sax, told me he never forgot this advice.

Eddie went to New York with drummer Ray Bauduc in 1929. Ben Pollock offered them jobs in his band, but he required Eddie to play tenor. Although Eddie had never touched a tenor sax, he learned to play it in a week and Pollock hired both men. Eddie and Ray later became charter members of the Bob Crosby band. Eddie was a fine clarinetist but rarely played that instrument after switching to tenor.

A friendly, outgoing man, he later returned to New Orleans and worked with Pete Fountain. Eddie played his first Gibson party in 1975, and I took a picture of him when he happened to be standing next to Bobby Hackett. Eddie just loved that photo.

As always, Eddie put everything he had into his playing during a 1976 gig by Pete Fountain's band at the jazz club in Jackson, Mississippi. I loved hearing Eddie reminisce about his days as a kid clarinet player in New Orleans.

Eddie had a steady gig on tenor sax with Pete Fountain in New Orleans during the '60s and '70s, and Pete would not let him off to play jazz parties. Pete made an exception in 1975 for Colorado Springs, where I took this photo of Eddie and Bobby Hackett, *left*.

Eddie enjoyed a reunion with Yank Lawson and Bud Freeman, *left and right,* when the World's Greatest Jazz
Band played a New Orleans club in 1974. He inscribed this photo to "Doc," my buddy, Robert Nixon.

Johnny Mince

Johnny and Pee Wee Erwin played together in Joe Haymes's orchestra in the early '30s. Johnny was an excellent clarinetist who doubled on all the reeds. He was featured on clarinet and alto sax in Tommy Dorsey's best bands of the late '30s and early '40s. I enjoyed his clarinet work, but I especially savored hearing him play baritone sax. On that instrument he reminded me of the great Ernie Caceres.

Like an excited teenager, Johnny was always full of enthusiasm. He told me that he seemed to have been born with the strong desire to be a musician. When his parents bought him his first clarinet, he wouldn't let it out of his sight. He even slept with it.

As a teenager playing his first professional job, Johnny was given a dark band uniform by the leader. The young clarinetist thought it would be a nice touch to wear a bright red sweater that his parents had given him. Johnny said he became the world's champion quick-change artist when the leader spotted him in that sweater.

I've never had more fun than the day Johnny, Pee Wee, and I found ourselves on the same plane going to one of the Gibson parties. They got out their horns, I mooched a tin plate and two long swizzle sticks from a flight attendant, and we played a fifteen-minute version of "Jazz Me Blues."

Johnny was a mainstay on clarinet and alto sax in Tommy Dorsey's best bands of the late '30s and early '40s. Johnny's playing reflected his bubbling personality. (Indianapolis, 1989)

Johnny played baritone sax during a set at the 1980 Odessa party. Kenny Davern stood to his right, and Pee Wee Erwin and George Masso to his left. Pee Wee died before I could ask him to sign this photo.

To Al
Regards
Bob Haggart

The Johnny Mince quartette
on their first Jazz party since
the album was made.
Thanks for the Picture Al
Cliff Leeman too! Johnny Mince

In 1979, Johnny made an excellent recording with, *left to right,* Lou Stein, Bob Haggart, and Cliff Leeman. It featured a stunning version of "The Man I Love."
(Odessa, 1981)

Michael Moore

Michael is not only a great bass player, but also one of those unique voices in jazz who has developed a sound very much his own. That sound, I believe, results from his playing the bass more like a guitarist than a bassist. I can't describe exactly what I see and hear when Michael is playing, but it reminds me of Hoagy Carmichael's comment when asked about the unique beauty of Bix Beiderbecke's sound. Hoagy said Bix's playing was like licorice: You've got to taste it to believe it.

Although a shy, soft-spoken man, Michael is a lot of fun to be around. His playing does not reflect his quiet personality.

I first heard Michael play at the Odessa party. He has a lot of respect for other fine musicians and was a bit awed by Milt Hinton and Jack Lesberg until they settled him down after a while. At the Conneaut Lake party, Michael hung over the piano and soaked up every note while Dave McKenna was playing solo.

Michael is one of a handful of world-class musicians who have developed their own individual voice on their instrument. No other bass player sounds like him, and he doesn't sound like any other. (Conneaut Lake, 1985)

At the 1985 Conneaut Lake party, Michael and Howard Alden, *left,* played a set together. These two masters produced some of the most beautiful jazz I have ever heard.

Michael played the Odessa party for the first time in 1981. His uniquely beautiful style knocked out everyone, including Milt Hinton, *right*.

Bennie Morton

Bennie was a fine trombone player from the Big Band Era, notably with Count Basie in the late '30s. He had previously played with big bands in New York during the '20s and early '30s, including those of Fletcher Henderson and Don Redman. I first heard Bennie at Dick Gibson's jazz parties of the early '70s and always loved his distinctive vibrato on the trombone.

In 1973, Ann and I went to New York so she could go to the theater and I could hear the World's Greatest Jazz Band. The WGJB, which included Bennie at that time, was playing at a club called the Half Note. Ann and I ran into Carolyn Scruggs, an old college girlfriend of mine, in the elevator at the Algonquin Hotel. The two women liked each other immediately and rushed off to see a play together.

I was more than a bit nervous because I didn't know what the two of them might tell each other about me. But Carolyn worked for the State Department and was headed for Africa the next day, so she and Ann didn't have time to chop me up into little pieces. The women and I met later at the Half Note, and my old friend asked me to request "Basin Street Blues," which Bennie called the "national anthem." He and the band thrilled her with the tune.

Bennie died in 1985. I heard him in the twilight of his career, and he never lost that beautiful vibrato.

I photographed Bennie while he was soloing on "Stardust" during a 1973 one-nighter in Alexandria, Louisiana, with the World's Greatest Jazz Band. This tune highlighted Bennie's unique trombone vibrato.

Bennie was a sweet, kind man. A shot of him with Benny Carter, *right,* at the Colorado Springs party in 1972 captured his friendly personality.

Every time the WGJB had a gig close enough to Pine Bluff, Robert Nixon and I went to hear the group. This photo shows Bennie with, *left to right,* Bob Wilber, Bud Freeman, Bob Haggart, Yank Lawson, and Gus Johnson at a joint on Bourbon Street in New Orleans in 1974.

Joe Muranyi

Joe combines his excellent musicianship on the clarinet and soprano sax with a puckish sense of humor. He calls me "The Organized Al White" because I file my photos of jazz musicians in labeled envelopes. He dubbed my wife "The Shy and Retiring Ann" because of her outgoing personality.

Joe worked at Jimmy Ryan's in New York with the great trumpet player Roy Eldridge until the famous jazz club was torn down to make room for another high-rise office building. After Roy retired, Joe worked a lot with Spanky Davis, another of my favorite trumpet players.

Ann and I met Joe while he was on tour with Yank Lawson and Bob Haggart playing a one-nighter at a small college in Mississippi. We spent the afternoon chatting with Joe, Al Klink, George Masso, and Bob and Yank. Joe is an excellent jazz singer, but the public address system was so bad that it drove him up the wall.

One year at the July 4th jazz party in Indianapolis, Joe called the old tune "Dardanella," featuring a special intro that he and the piano player, Eddie Higgins, had worked out years before in Chicago. Unfortunately, Eddie couldn't remember his part. They gave up after the fourth try. For the rest of the night, every musician delighted the audience by playing a quote from "Dardanella" during each of his solos.

Joe has played clarinet and soprano sax in New York's best jazz spots. He's also an entertaining vocalist, and the patter that he carries on with audiences adds to the fun of jazz. (Indianapolis, 1988)

The front line of any jazz band is lucky to include Joe and the fine trumpet player Spanky Davis, *left*. They posed together at the Indianapolis party in 1991.

Joe stood between Roy Eldridge, *left,* and Bobby Pratt during a gig at Jimmy Ryan's in 1978.
He worked on and off in the famous New York club for several years.

Turk Murphy

San Francisco was always home base for Turk, but he brought his band to several jazz parties through the years. He blew his trombone in a distinctively rough style, reminding me of Dick Wellstood's belief that jazz should be played with a little grease and funk. Turk played with a lot of both.

Turk, like Jim Cullum today, always had a well-rehearsed band. He didn't limit himself to standard tunes but dug into the history of jazz and came up with some great old numbers, among them rags and blues. Turk spoke with a stutter, but there was no sign of it when he sang. A quiet, reserved man, he did a lot to keep the old jazz alive.

Turk Murphy—Just for the Record is an interesting book by Jim Goggin, based on his verbatim interviews with Turk.

Turk had a long career playing trombone in and around San Francisco, mostly as a leader, from the early '40s until his death in 1987. He stuttered but had no trouble singing the old jazz tunes. Turk owned his own club, Earthquake McGoon's, where I snapped him in 1974. Pete Clute is on piano.

This photo shows several members of Turk's band during the '70s. Turk is playing a trombone feature called "I Am Pecan Pete," along with, *left to right,* Bob Helm, Leon Oakley, Bill Carroll (on trombone), and Pete Clute. (St. Louis, 1974)

Turk's vocal on "Evolution Mama" featured this little jig. He appears here with Bob Helm, Leon Oakley, Carl Lunsford, Bill Carroll (partially obscured on tuba), and Pete Clute, *left to right*. (St. Louis, 1974)

Marty Napoleon

Marty is a powerful piano player who attacks the keyboard with everything he has. Whenever I hear him play, he borrows my emery board after every set to file the thick calluses on his fingers. Cotton buyers always carry an emery board because they pick up calluses from handling the fibers. Marty has a happy personality, always wears a big smile, and hates to see a musician loaf or look sour on the stand. His uncle, Phil Napoleon, played trumpet and formed the Original Memphis Five.

Marty tells funny stories, some of which come from his days in the big bands and at Condon's. One night after a gig, he and the other members of the Condon gang began arguing about who had the longest nose they had ever seen. Brad Gowans, the great valve trombonist, bet that the honor belonged to a shopkeeper in a town in upstate New York. Others insisted otherwise. They all piled into a car and took off to measure the guy's nose.

At about 4 a.m., the musicians arrived and woke up the merchant's whole family, who lived above the store. While Brad held a ruler to the man's nose, the poor fellow kept yelling for his wife to call the police. Although the musicians were soberer than when they left Condon's, no one remembers who won the bet.

Marty, a fine percussive pianist, played the jazz parts in the 1930s movies made by the band of Chico Marx of the Marx Brothers. He was a member of Pee Wee Erwin's band that played at my 50th birthday party in 1978 and then for the jazz society of Jackson, Mississippi, where I took this picture.

On the trip from Pine Bluff to Jackson in 1978, we stopped for lunch in Vicksburg. Marty and Pee Wee Erwin, *left,* spotted this old jukebox that had some of their records, and we heard some great music with our hamburgers.

I don't believe I've ever seen Marty when he wasn't smiling. He and Lou Stein, *left,* had a ball playing a hot duet at the 1985 Odessa party.

Red Norvo

Red made a jazz instrument of the xylophone, and later the vibraharp, when the Paul Whiteman orchestra featured him in the late '20s and early '30s. He played at several of the Odessa jazz parties, and I had an incomparable experience chatting with Red about Bix Beiderbecke and the other early greats with whom he had performed.

The idea of the Benny Goodman Trio was hatched at a party at the home of Red and his wife, vocalist Mildred Bailey. Benny and Teddy Wilson were guests, and Mildred suggested that they play together with her cousin, Carl Bellinger, an amateur drummer.

Red played beautifully at the Odessa parties. He was often featured in vibraharp-piano duets with Dave McKenna. Red had a special arrangement on vibes of Beiderbecke's "In a Mist." When he played it, the proverbial pin could be heard dropping in the audience.

Although unable to play after suffering a stroke, Red attended several parties in a wheelchair. He kept his great sense of humor and the twinkle in his eye.

Red could not travel to the March of Jazz party in 1997. However, jazz writer Floyd Levin went to his home and made a tape of him thanking the audience for wishing him a happy birthday. Red still had the twinkle. He died two years later.

In a slapstick routine on the old song "Ida," Red signaled Cliff Leeman, *right,* with his elbow and then tried to mix him up. Jack Lesberg was on bass with the two of them for a set at the Odessa party in 1975.

Red sometimes used large felt-covered mallets, which gave the vibes a uniquely beautiful sound. He called them "Idahos on a stick" when autographing this photo at the 1975 Colorado Springs party.

Red suffered a stroke in 1995 and could not play at the March of Jazz the next year. However, he enjoyed the music with a childhood friend. The musicians behind them were, *left to right,* Bob Wilber, Joe Bushkin, Flip Phillips, Dave Frishberg, Bob Haggart, and Dick Hyman, all of whom had a March birthday. (Clearwater, 1996)

Ken Peplowski

Ken is superb on both clarinet and tenor sax. He plays a specialty on clarinet at a breakneck tempo with "Ring Dem Bells" that ranks as one of my most exciting musical treats. It's on a Concord CD, but hearing and watching Ken play it in a live performance is unforgettable.

Ken's mischievousness goes with his quick wit. He's always up to something on the stand. Ken and Dan Barrett like to wait until the final set of a party to pull some of the most outrageous high jinks imaginable, with corny joke routines and outlandish costumes and makeup. Sometimes they swap horns, presenting a tableau of two musicians looking as serious as possible while performing an especially difficult arrangement.

One evening, Howard Alden and Bucky Pizzarelli were playing a two-guitar number. Ken suddenly grabbed Bucky's guitar and announced that *he* would solo with Howard. Fine, said Bucky and Howard. But Ken refused to take a guitar solo when Howard nodded to him to do so. He just stood there, avidly going through the motions of providing rhythm backup. "You take it," he kept telling a frustrated Howard, to the delight of the audience. Ken finally wound up in Bucky's lap "playing" the guitar with Bucky actually doing the playing, his arms stretched around Ken's body.

The antics of these three master musicians brought down the house.

Ken and Dan Barrett, *right,* love to pull ridiculous stunts on the stand. Looking as serious and innocent as possible, they switched horns at the 1989 Indianapolis party.

Ken plays great jazz equally beautifully on clarinet and tenor sax. He started out with the Tommy Dorsey band led by Buddy Morrow, who recalled that Ken never failed to get a standing ovation after being featured on a tune. (Atlanta, 1992)

At the 1989 Conneaut Lake party, Ken, accompanied by Bucky Pizzarelli, *left,* and Gene Estes, played several of the old Benny Goodman numbers.

Flip Phillips

This great musician gives everything he has whenever he's on the stand. Flip's tenor sax solos on chorus after chorus at breakneck tempos are legendary. As Frank Tate says, "Flip takes no prisoners." The solemn bowing routine between Flip and Howard Alden that closes the lovely "Poor Butterfly" is also a favorite at jazz parties.

At one party, while playing a beautiful ballad, Flip spotted a man reading a book at the table in front of him. He stopped at the end of a phrase, leaned down, and told the guy to either listen or go somewhere else and read. The guy closed the book. Flip continued the tune without missing a beat.

I love to hear Flip play the mellow bass clarinet, which he rarely does. Although he seldom plays his regular clarinet either, he is a fine clarinetist.

Years ago, Flip and Ralph Sutton, close friends who are artists of few words and much music, came up with nicknames for each other. Flip calls Ralph *Harry,* and Ralph calls Flip *Skip.* Neither has any idea why they do so.

Rachel and Mat Domber, *left,* put on a March of Jazz in Deerfield Beach in 1995 celebrating Flip's 80th birthday. The Dombers founded Arbors Records and have produced some of the finest jazz recordings in history.

I have never seen Flip dog it on the stand. He gives all he's got in every performance. Flip and trombonist Bill Harris were my favorite musicians in Woody Herman's famous First Herd in 1946. (Odessa, 1985)

Flip played a set with Bob Wilber and Kenny Davern, *center and right,* at the 1994 March of Jazz in St. Petersburg. In 1977, Flip and Kenny made a terrific album together called *John* (Kenny) *and Joe* (Flip).

Bucky Pizzarelli

Bucky plays a seven-string guitar, enabling him to hit lovely low notes that most guitarists can't reach. His playing sounds like the guitar contains a bass. Bucky is unsurpassed as a rhythm guitarist, and his solos are extraordinarily beautiful. I've heard him play Django Reinhardt's "Nuages" countless times, but it never fails to grab me.

One of my fondest jazz party memories is the night after hours in Odessa when Bucky and Kenny Davern sat on a balcony above the pool and played duets for more than an hour. It was gorgeous.

Bucky's son, John, Jr., is almost as popular on guitar and also has had a successful singing career. His playing on Bucky's CD "Nirvana" for CDC earned this paternal comment: "Thanks to my son, John, for that superb rhythm and choice harmonic solos on Nuages and Azure'te. Plus a blazing single string solo (ala George Barnes) on Honeysuckle Rose—and, most of all, the guitar duets (family style)."

Affable and soft spoken, Bucky always seems to wear a big smile. When he gives my wife, Ann, a kiss on the cheek, she doesn't wash her face for a week.

Bucky and Milt Hinton, *right,* have teamed up at a large number of jazz parties and on dozens of my favorite recordings. What a beat they lay down in the rhythm section! (Wilmington, 1986)

Bucky, a peerless rhythm guitarist, loves to play and seems never to tire. He's also a marvelous soloist, and his enthusiasm comes through in his music. (Kingsport, 1994)

During an after-hours session at the 1995 Odessa party, Bucky was flanked by Dan Barrett, *left,* and Jack Lesberg. As usual, he was happy to continue playing after working several sets before a large audience. Bucky also enjoyed watching Dan use his foot to maneuver the slide of his trombone.

Ed Polcer

I first met Ed when he arrived for the 1975 Odessa party. He had been recommended for the gig by Pee Wee Erwin, and over the intervening years he has become one of my closest friends.

At that time, Ed played cornet at Condon's and also was the manager of the club. However, some of the musicians at the party in Odessa had never played with him. As a result, Ed took the stand, called the first tune, and gave the tempo—and no one played a note. Ralph Sutton looked up at him from the piano and said, "I'll set the tempo." Ed, though startled, understood what had happened. Ralph quickly recognized the caliber of Ed's playing, and the two have been the best of friends ever since.

Ann and I heard Ed and Vic Dickenson together at Condon's several times, and those two put on a great show. Ed has brought groups to play in Pine Bluff, surrounding himself with such top players as Cliff Leeman, John Bunch, Bobby Gordon, Allan Vaché, and Tom Artin. Ed and Tom knew each other at Princeton, where Ed earned an engineering degree and played cornet professionally. He was a member of the Tiger Town Five, which played at Grace Kelly's wedding in Monaco.

Ed knocks me out with his choice of tunes and the way he directs traffic on the stand. It's fun hearing him use the old Condon tricks—the stop-time solo, the key change on the out chorus, and the four-bar wail by each instrument at the end of a number. His horn has a pulsating, keep-it-going drive that never lags. How I wish there was still a spot like Condon's in New York.

There's a great front line in this photo of Ed flanked by Allan Vaché, *left,* and Dan Barrett. Ed played cornet at Condon's and also managed the club. (Odessa, 1996)

Ed posed backstage with Kenny Davern and Milt Hinton, *center and right,* at a school gig during the Odessa party in 1982. The musicians took their time explaining the music to the kids and answering questions.

At the Conneaut Lake party in 1983, Ed greeted Joe Slovac, *right,* a physician and jazz clarinetist who was a guest. Bob Havens sat to their right. The apparent gray streak in Ed's hair came from my camera's flash.

Randy Reinhart

Randy blows beautiful jazz on both trombone and trumpet. He played trombone in Jim Cullum's band for more than ten years, and Jim also featured him frequently on cornet.

I particularly enjoyed hearing Randy play duets with John Sheridan, the band's pianist. They remained close friends after Randy left Cullum and have performed together at the Conneaut Lake, Pennsylvania, party. Randy and John enjoy playing such old, obscure tunes as "Oh, Baby, Don't Say No, Say Maybe" and "Learn to Croon." Randy is an excellent reader as well as a fine improviser. I have seen him run down a new arrangement by Dan Barrett or Keith Ingham and then play it perfectly the first time through.

Randy likes to tell about the time he drove to the home of Spiegle Wilcox north of New York in the middle of winter. Deep snow lay everywhere. Randy had a nice visit with the elderly trombonist, who was born in 1903 and played with Bix Beiderbecke in the 1928 orchestra of Gene Goldkette. Driving from Spiegle's home, Randy got stuck in a ditch and walked back for assistance. Out came the 92-year-old Spiegle in a four-wheel drive. Using a winch, he rescued Randy and sent him on his way.

Randy, a versatile musician who plays both trombone and trumpet, was a member of Jim Cullum's band when I took this photo. He played trombone with Jim but was often featured on cornet as well. (St. Louis, 1986)

Randy's close friend, John Sheridan, looks at him attentively from the piano as they play a duet. (Conneaut Lake, 1994)

Ken Peplowski, *left,* and Bob Havens flanked Randy for a set at the Conneaut Lake party in 1989.
Isla Eckinger, *far left,* was on bass.

Scott Robinson

One of the most versatile musicians I have ever heard, Scott specializes on reed instruments. He's great on clarinet and tenor sax, and especially on baritone sax. He's also terrific on trumpet and trombone. When Scott first hit New York, he made a jazz band recording on which he played all the parts except the rhythm section.

Scott has learned from the masters while putting his own stamp on the music. He searched the junk shops in Hot Springs and found some old 78s featuring Flip Phillips, plus a mint condition Smithsonian reissue of the early big bands.

Before meeting Scott, I asked Marty Grosz to tell me what he looked like. Marty said to picture Ichabod Crane of the Washington Irving story, "The Legend of Sleepy Hollow." Sure enough, Scott is a tall, thin beanpole—but he eats like a horse. We had lunch at a joint in Hot Springs that prides itself on red beans and rice, and always serves more than anyone can eat. I ate half of mine and was about to burst, but Scott finished it after cleaning his own plate.

Two young Turks of the tenor sax, Scott, *left,* and Harry Allen, *right,* expressed deep appreciation for this shot of themselves with one of the old masters, Flip Phillips. (Clearwater, 1996)

Scott, shown with Frank Tate on bass, plays all the reed instruments. He's playing tenor sax here, but I especially like to hear him on baritone sax. Scott also owns a contrabass sax, the woodwind with the lowest pitch. (Waterloo Village, 1996)

To Al White!

[signature]

Ed Polcer led a band on a tour of Community Concerts in Arkansas, and Scott played a couple of the gigs because Ken Peplowski had a conflict. Mark Shane is on piano in this photo. (Hot Springs, 1994)

Bobby Rosengarden

I took some of my earliest photos of Bobby when he was playing drums with Pee Wee Erwin at one of Dick Gibson's jazz parties in Colorado Springs in the early 1970s. Bobby had an eye for a pretty girl, and Pee Wee always introduced him as the band's sex symbol whenever they worked together.

One of my pictures of Bobby at a Gibson party shows him playing a noon set with Bobby Hackett after being up almost all night. He wrote on the photo, "Dear Al, you now have proof that Jews drink."

Bobby worked on the old *Tonight Show* and later became musical director of *The Dick Cavett Show.* He told me that he and Milt Hinton formed part of the Nairobi Trio on *The Ernie Kovacs Show,* wearing ape suits. Bobby and Milt later joined with pianist Derek Smith in a combo called simply The Trio. They made some fine recordings.

A great entertainer, Bobby often blows a police whistle in rhythm when performing a solo. He is an excellent bongo player and his feature on bongos with the Duke Ellington tune "Caravan" has been a crowd pleaser for years.

Bobby was the drummer with Kenny Davern and Bob Wilber on the first recordings by Soprano Summit. He and Kenny, together with Dick Wellstood on piano, formed the Blue Three. One night during a tour in England, Bobby got furious with Kenny and Dick about something and walked out. Kenny took the mike and told the audience, "Now, folks, you're going to hear the Blue Two."

Robert Nixon and I first met Bobby at Dick Gibson's jazz party in 1971. Since then, when he spots us at a party he yells, "Let me at them drums!" (Colorado Springs, 1973)

Bobby, a gifted bongo player, is shown here with Bucky Pizzarelli at a school gig during the 1978 Odessa party. He has a trick of wetting his finger and drawing it across the head of the larger drum to produce a glissando sound. Milt Hinton would shout, "Bobby, are you calling me?"

Bobby's bubbling personality shines through in his drumming. During a feature number, he often blows a shrill police whistle in rhythm. (Colorado Springs, 1974)

Randy Sandke

Randy is one of the most gifted trumpet players I have ever heard. He has excellent control on both the highest and lowest notes. Randy soloed on "I Can't Get Started" one night at the Odessa party, and everyone in the hall knew he had barely hit that last high note. "Now you know where the expression 'by the skin of your teeth' comes from," he told the crowd.

I'm always impressed by the respect Randy has for his audience. When he is the leader of a set, he announces the name of the tune. Then he introduces the soloists and says a little about them.

Randy tells a story about the night he was picked up late for a gig being played by a Woody Herman-type band. He had already unpacked his horn in the car by the time they arrived at the place where the band was performing. The trumpet players had started blasting away on the first number as Randy rushed to the top of the stand. A big dinner was being held in the adjacent room, separated from the band by a heavy curtain directly behind the musicians. When Randy reached the trumpet section, he took one step too many, pulled down the curtain, and landed in the next room.

I wonder if the people at that dinner are still pondering the flying trumpet player.

Randy, one of the finest all-around jazz trumpet players of his day, is quiet and unassuming. But can he blow! Randy is very considerate of the audience and, when leading a set, always announces the name of each tune. (Odessa, 1995)

This photo shows Randy watching Jon-Erik Kellso and Dan Barrett, *center and right,* during the heat of improvisation. As leader of the trumpet trio, he is about to signal them on his horn. (Indianapolis, 1995)

Following the 1994 Jerome Jazz in Aspen, Randy and his wife, Karen, *third from left,* relaxed with
Dick and Julia Hyman. Jack Lesberg and Ralph Sutton can be seen at the table in the background.

Gray Sargent

Gray is a fine guitar player from the Cape Cod area. He works a lot with Dave McKenna, who also lives there. Many of the top jazz musicians of the East Coast come up to the Boston vicinity to play with Gray.

I first heard Gray at the jazz party in Conneaut Lake, Pennsylvania, in 1987. Dave was also at that party, and listening to them play together was a thrill.

At the Triangle party in Kingsport, Tennessee, in 1996, Gray did a set at a local high school with Jackie Coon, the flugelhorn player, and vocalist Becky Kilgore. They performed and lectured for a roomful of students, and Gray made the trio sound like an orchestra. The three professionals patiently answered the kids' questions about jazz and helped broaden their knowledge about the music.

Gray became Tony Bennet's guitarist in 1996, but he still makes some jazz parties.

Gray, together with Becky Kilgore and Jackie Coon, *center and right,* had a lot of fun playing a gig for high school band students bussed in from three cities during the 1996 Kingsport party.

Gray, a world-class guitarist and a native of New England, has spent most of his career in the Boston area. (Conneaut Lake, 1990)

I love to hear Gray and his fellow New Englander, Dave McKenna, *left,* play the great arrangements they have worked out together. If Dave is playing a solo set and Gray is in the house, he'll invite his friend to join him after a few tunes. (Kingsport, 1996)

Tom Saunders

Tom, an exciting cornet player and excellent showman, leads a group called the Wild Bill Davison Legacy. Wild Bill was his boyhood hero, and Tom became Bill's chief disciple. Tommy hung around Bill so much that there's no telling what he'll say to an audience from the stand. He served as host and interviewer on a fine video, *Wild Bill Davison*, which tells the story of Bill's life.

At several jazz parties I have heard Tom play with Chuck Hedges, one of Wild Bill's favorite clarinetists, and trombonist Bill Allred. They make up a powerful front line.

Tom's wife, Tillie, is German. He says he had to learn German to comprehend the names she was calling him. During a tour of Germany with Yank Lawson, Yank locked his key in his room and could not make the desk clerk understand what had happened. Tom came along and translated the problem. He was so proud of himself that he called his wife and announced that he was now Yank's official German interpreter. Tillie hooted over the phone, "Both of you are in deep trouble."

Tom is the heir apparent to Wild Bill Davison. He is his own man on cornet but worked a lot with Bill and learned much from him. After Spanky Davis, *right,* played an exceptional trumpet solo, Tom asked me, "How in hell did he do that?" (Indianapolis, 1987)

A band including, *left to right,* Chuck Hedges, Bill Allred, Bob Haggart, and Tom played one of the finest sets at the 1987 Indianapolis party.

When posing with Ann, Tom wore a shirt that his wife, Tillie, had given him. Tillie is German, and Tommy claims he had to learn her language to know what she was calling him. (Los Angeles, 1991)

Mark Shane

Mark is one of the best of the younger piano players. When he was first trying to get started around New York, Mona Hinton gave him some good advice: "You're going to have to learn to use your left hand if you're going to make it in jazz." Mark did just that and developed into an outstanding two-handed pianist. He's also an excellent singer.

Like Keith Ingham, Mark is always searching for old songs that not only are good but haven't been played to death. He has performed in Pine Bluff with Ed Polcer, and I love to hear him play those old tunes just for himself after hours. Mark shares my interest in photography and does his own dark-room work.

At the Wilmington, North Carolina, party in 1999, I got a big kick out of Mark's wife, Alice, who sat in on piano and accompanied herself singing the blues.

Mark is a clever vocalist as well as one of the top young pianists. This photo was taken in 1996 in Fayetteville, Arkansas, where he was playing a gig with Terry Blaine, the fine singer with whom Mark has worked for years.

I took this picture in my living room while Mark was on tour in 1993 with a band led by Ed Polcer. The musicians stayed with us and the Nixons. After dinner, Mark sat down at our piano and played "Honey Hush," one of my favorite Fats Waller tunes.

Terry Blaine, *left,* posed with Mark at the Atlanta party in 1994. The two of them have recorded several excellent CDs together.

John Sheridan

John is the superb pianist and arranger of the Jim Cullum Jazz Band. He loves arranging even more than playing. John points out that if a musician plays a great but unrecorded chorus, no one will ever hear it again. However, if the chorus had been written down, it could be preserved. John writes arrangements without the need of a piano.

For my 70th birthday party in February 1998, I engaged a band that included Bob Haggart, who wrote "South Rampart Street Parade," on bass. John wrote an arrangement of this grand old tune for jazz band and symphony orchestra, and the band played it with the Pine Bluff Symphony. He was thrilled that Bob was one of the first to play the arrangement with an orchestra.

I have heard John play piano duets with such masters as Dick Hyman, Dave McKenna, and Ralph Sutton, and he can hold his own with any of them. In fact, Ralph invited John to play an unscheduled two-piano encore set with him at the 1993 Summit Jazz in Denver. It was the first time Ralph had done that with any pianist.

John has been a mainstay of the Jim Cullum Jazz Band since 1979. He excels both at the piano and as an arranger. (Conneaut Lake, 1989)

John loves every chance he gets to work with Ralph Sutton, *left*. Ralph has been an inspiration to him through the years. (Pensacola, 1990)

Another of John's favorite pianists is Dave McKenna, *left*. John suggested that Dave play a gig with the Cullum band in San Antonio, but Dave told him, "Jim has all he needs in a piano player." (Conneaut Lake, 1994)

Ray Sherman

One of my favorite albums of all time is *This Is Teagarden,* which Jack made shortly before his death. Ray was the pianist for this recording date, and Jack told him to play as much as he wanted throughout the album. Ray certainly did.

Ray's playing is always crisp and clean. It reminds me of Jess Stacy's, with the distinctive tremolo in the right hand.

Ray, a rather quiet, reserved man, has spent most of his career on the West Coast, where he has done a wide range of movie work, recording, and jazz gigs. He was the pianist in that grand old film *Pete Kelly's Blues,* starring Jack Webb, Ella Fitzgerald, and Peggy Lee.

Whenever I'm at a party where Ray is one of the musicians, I try to get together for dinner with Ray and his wife, Jeannie. It's fun to hear him and other veterans reminisce about the old days in jazz. Ray, whose father was a bandleader in Chicago, heard all the great early players as a young man.

Ray is a fine West Coast piano player who has spent most of his career in jazz clubs and the movie industry. His piano was featured in *Pete Kelly's Blues,* a film about jazz musicians in the '20s. (Odessa, 1993)

Here's a shot of two more of my favorite pianists, Ray and Joe Bushkin, *left.* Ray makes effective use of the right-hand tremolo that Jess Stacy employed so well. (Clearwater, 1996)

I love to listen to old-time jazz musicians reminisce about their careers. Ray got together with Bob Haggart and reedman Rosy McHargue, *left and center,* in Los Angeles in 1995.

Zoot Sims

Zoot was a marvelous, exciting player in any idiom of jazz. The first time I heard him play tenor sax was when Woody Herman had a one-nighter in Springfield, Missouri, in 1949. My jazz buddies and I went up to hear the band. In those days, Zoot signed his autograph "Jack Sims," but could he play!

Dave Frishberg wrote a clever song as a tribute to Zoot. According to the lyrics, when Zoot came in and unpacked his horn, all the people in the hall would be wise to call home and tell the folks not to expect them until late. It was going to be a long night with him playing. That's how musicians and jazz fans alike felt about Zoot.

At one of Dick Gibson's parties in Colorado Springs, I was listening to Zoot with Clive Acker. Zoot looked like he had been up all night, and his sax had absolutely no lacquer left on it after all the years on the road. "Poor Zoot," Clive said sarcastically. "He must have stayed up all night polishing his horn." After the set we kidded Zoot about his sax. "You guys better not get near my horn," he told us. "It's got syphilis."

Zoot was one of the finest tenor sax players that America has produced. Despite being a heavy drinker, he never let it interfere with his music and always sounded wonderful. (Colorado Springs, 1977)

Zoot played soprano sax in a set with Joe Venuti and Major Holley, *left and center,* at the Colorado Springs party in 1976. Joe loved playing duets with Zoot and would shout, "Where's my Zootie?"

During the '50s. and '60s, Zoot and Al Cohn, *center,* made jazz history with their exciting tenor sax duets. Slam Stewart is on bass. (Colorado Springs, 1978)

Derek Smith

Derek is an English pianist who has been playing in the United States even longer than Keith Ingham, having moved over here after World War II. During the war, he sought out American jazz musicians who were stationed in the Army in England. They included Major Holley, one of my favorite bass players, who taught Derek a lot about jazz.

In 1985, a Japanese recording company hired Derek to make an album in Japan with George Duvivier, another of my favorite bassists, and Gus Johnson. During the flight over, they chose about a dozen tunes for the album. However, upon arriving at the recording studio, Derek was informed that the company had made its own selection of tunes, none of which was even remotely associated with jazz.

Derek, George, and Gus decided not to argue, but to take the money and run. They struggled with the odd assortment of music for about twelve hours. When the time came to record the last number, Derek asked for the music and was told there was none. A child would sing it for them.

The Japanese youngster sang a little two-bar phrase for the musicians to turn into an entire track for the recording. They decided to follow George's suggestion and play the phrase as a blues and get out of there. The resulting tune, "Aki Tumbo" ("Little Butterfly"), became the number one hit in Japan and also had a good run in the United States.

As a studio pianist during his early days in New York, Derek's schedule often included recording in the morning, then taping the *Tonight Show* with Doc Severinson's band, and finishing up with Benny Goodman at night. Derek moved to the United States from England after World War II at the age of twenty-six. (St. Louis, 1994)

Derek's playing, according to Milt Hinton, *right,* sounds as though he has fifteen fingers. In the background of this photo, Robert Nixon is chatting with Margaret Gillum, an avid jazz fan from Odessa who helps put on the party there. (St. Louis, 1995)

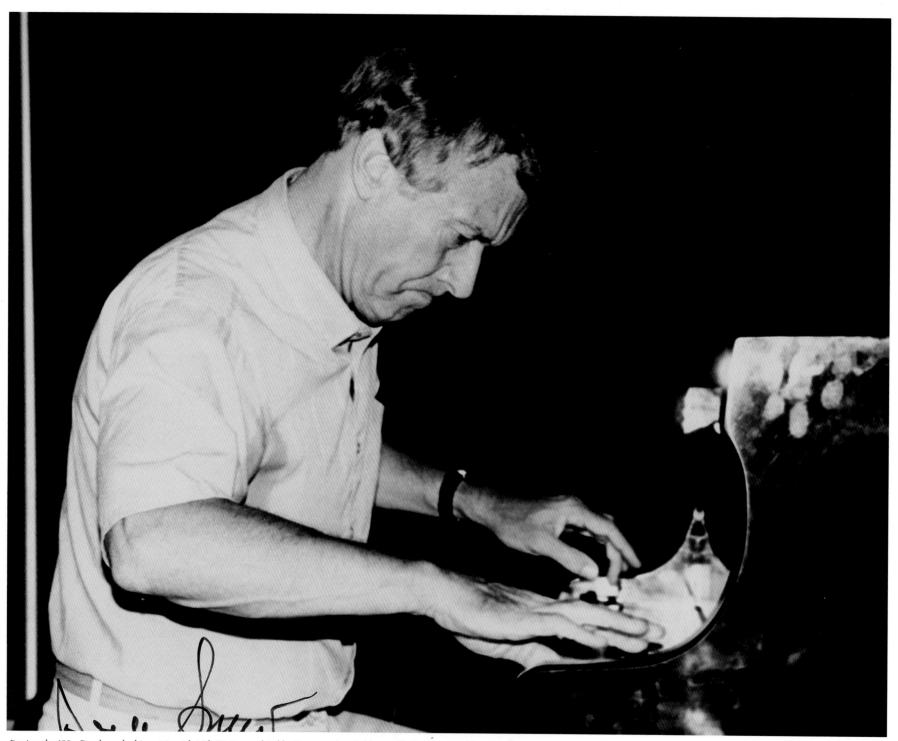

During the '80s, Derek worked in a trio with Milt Hinton and Bobby Rosengarden. Bobby recalls that they would arrive for an early morning recording date after working the night before, and the studio remained quiet until Derek started "kicking them in the ass" with his piano playing. (Indianapolis, 1990)

Jess Stacy

Jess's marvelous style of jazz piano featured a distinctive tremolo in his right hand. He has been one of my favorite pianists for as long as I can remember. I met Jess at a jazz party in Sacramento, California, in 1976. Unfortunately, we never got together again, though we corresponded until his death.

The photo of Jess in his high school yearbook in Cape Girardeau, Missouri, had a caption that said, "He thrives on Jazz." Jess played on riverboats and then in Chicago before joining Benny Goodman's band. He became known for a delightful, unscheduled, and highly unusual solo near the end of "Sing, Sing, Sing" during the historic Goodman concert at Carnegie Hall in 1938. After finishing his own solo, Benny surprised Jess completely by signaling him to take one. Jess sure did just that.

Jess's piano also was a highlight of the Bob Crosby band and Crosby's Bob Cats. He married Lee Wiley, my favorite singer.

Jess and Ralph Sutton, both noted for their superb comping, or supportive (complementary) playing behind soloists, were good friends. Jess once told Ralph, "I love music but I hate to play it."

Derek Coller wrote an excellent biography, *Jess Stacy, The Quiet Man of Jazz*.

Jess is one of my all-time favorites in the world of jazz. He had been retired from music for several years before I heard him play at a party in Sacramento in 1976. It was a thrill to meet the immortal pianist and his wife, Pat.

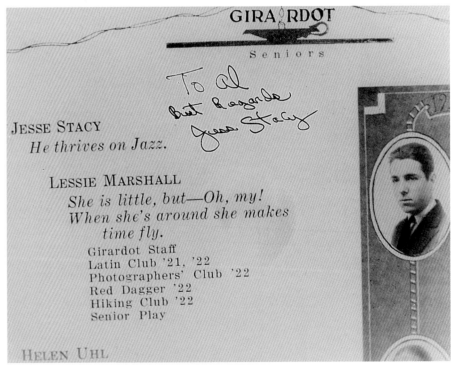

In the 1970s, I played trombone in a band that included eight females—six guitarists, a piano player, and a drummer. One of those guitarists, Eddie Maupin (who is still going strong at 95) was a classmate of Jess's and let me copy this from her yearbook and send it to Jess for his autograph.

The night I took this picture of Jess, he had to work with a group that included a very modern rock drummer; thus the stern expression. (Sacramento, 1976)

Lou Stein

Lou is a fine East Coast piano player whose first big job was playing in Glenn Miller's final band in the early '40s. He did a lot of work with Ray McKinley after the war and played on the Lawson-Haggart Jazz Band records of the '50s.

Lou was one of the first pianists to play the Odessa jazz parties, and through the years I saw him at many other parties. One year he brought his son, Alex, to Odessa with him, and my son, Al III, came with me. The two boys were the same age and had a great time listening to the music and hanging out together.

In 1986, Lou came to Pine Bluff to play a solo concert at the Arts Center. He stayed at our home, and before the concert Lou and I polished off about a pint of rocky road ice cream. In the middle of his concert, Lou started to play an original slow blues. "Folks," he told the audience, "I am making this up as I go along. The title is 'Rocky Road,' and it's dedicated to Al White, who is fifty-eight years old today."

I like this shot of Lou with the Steinway logo on the piano. Carl Fontana used to yell "Steinway!" after Lou had played an exciting solo. (Odessa, 1981)

All the top piano players loved Teddy Wilson, *left,* and Lou was no exception. As Lou and I were entering the hotel restaurant for dinner at the 1984 Odessa party, he spotted Teddy and asked me to take this picture.

When Lou ripped off an especially good solo and the audience responded with boisterous applause, he stood up and showed his appreciation like this. Milt Hinton, *right,* agreed with the audience. (Odessa, 1975)

Maxine Sullivan

Maxine had the most relaxed delivery of all the vocalists I have ever heard. When I first heard her, at the Conneaut Lake Jazz Party in 1975, she worked with a rhythm section and one horn playing behind her.

Ed Polcer and his cornet backed Maxine on her first set at that party, and he asked a very young Bob Reitmeier to do the second set with her. Bob was extremely nervous about playing with Maxine and could hardly go on the stand. But his clarinet sounded so good backing Maxine that he played all her other sets as well.

Maxine was very popular during the late '30s and early '40s. She worked with and married bassist John Kirby, who had a fine sextet featuring such luminaries as Charlie Shavers on trumpet and Billy Kyle on piano. She later married Cliff Jackson, another top pianist. Maxine didn't work much during the late '50s and early '60s, but she returned to the scene with the World's Greatest Jazz Band in the early '70s. She also sang at some of Dick Gibson's jazz parties and recorded with Bob Wilber and Scott Hamilton.

Maxine sometimes got her audience to join her on such tunes as "Goody Goody" and "We Just Couldn't Say Goodbye." When Bob Reitmeier was accompanying her and stepped up to play a chorus, she would turn and tell him, "Say something."

I loved to hear Maxine sing the blues. She had worked with Louis Armstrong at the Cotton Club and learned from him. Maxine's timing and phrasing were so relaxed and natural that to me they sounded perfect. (Conneaut Lake, 1984)

Maxine made some excellent records during the '80s. with Bob Reitmeier, *left,* a fine West Coast clarinet player. When Bob first accompanied Maxine, in 1975, he was so nervous that he had trouble going up to the stand. (Conneaut Lake, 1985)

This was the last picture I took of Maxine. She died about six months later before I could ask her to autograph it. Milt Hinton, *left,* said it all in his inscription: "What a lady." (Wilmington, 1987)

Ralph Sutton

In 1952, while in the Army at Fort Devens, Massachusetts, I spent several weekends in New York and always went to Eddie Condon's club. Wild Bill Davison, Cutty Cutshall, and Edmond Hall made up the wonderful front line, but Ralph Sutton, the intermission piano player, knocked me out.

Ralph is the chief disciple of Fats Waller's rollicking stride piano style. To me, Ralph's playing represents a distillation of pure jazz. He is the most exciting musician I have ever heard on up-tempo numbers. Yet, I believe his music reaches its most thrilling and beautiful peak on the Bix Beiderbecke piano solos, "In a Mist," "In the Dark," "Flashes," and "Candlelights."

Ann and I have had a thing going with Ralph for many years. He is our marriage counselor.

Robert and Janey Nixon's daughter, Lyn, got married in 1976, and Ralph, Dick Cary, Jack Lesberg, and Gus Johnson came to Pine Bluff for her wedding. They played at the reception and again the next day at the city's Arts Center and a private party.

I chased around after the musicians and paid little attention to Ann. When the weekend was over, she walked up to Ralph and me while we were chatting. "Well, Mr. White," my wife said, "I'm glad to finally see you." Ralph, in his most conciliatory manner, replied, "Ann, cut out that fucking shit." Since then, whenever Ann and I have a spat, I tell her, "Honey, I'm going to call our marriage counselor."

Jim Shacter, the coauthor of this book, has written a fine biography of Ralph called *Loose Shoes*.

Here are the Last of the Whorehouse Piano Players, Ralph and Jay McShann, *right*. These two artists love and respect each other, and they get a tremendous kick playing together on two pianos. (St. Louis, 1984)

Ralph is the master stride piano player. His left hand is an amazing powerhouse of rhythm. Ralph plays the Fats Waller and Bix Beiderbecke tunes better than anyone else. (St. Louis, 1996)

Ralph swung through "Ring Dem Bells" for Jim and Nancy Shacter at the 10th and final Jerome Jazz held in Aspen, in 1998. Ralph and his wife, Sunnie, announced that they would continue the party in Denver, beginning in 2000. When Dick Gibson gave his first jazz party, at the Hotel Jerome in Aspen in 1963, Ralph was the first musician he invited to play at the affair.

Barbara Sutton Curtis, *right,* Ralph's sister, is a top jazz pianist in her own right. She and Ralph perform on two pianos at parties and concerts. Barbara and Jim Shacter, Ralph's biographer and my collaborator on this book, clowned with him at the 1984 party in Menlo Park, California.

Buddy Tate

Buddy grew up in Texas and became a star of the Count Basie band, playing tenor sax and doubling on clarinet. I first heard him at one of Dick Gibson's parties in the early '70s and still remember a set he played with Flip Phillips that wowed the audience.

In 1981, Buddy fainted while taking a hot shower and was burned severely. He received a letter from a convict at Cummins prison, near my home in Pine Bluff, Arkansas, that helped make him fight to recover and start playing his horn again. The convict was behind bars for life and had heard Buddy on a radio show out of St. Louis.

"My life is over," the prisoner wrote, "but if you are the Buddy Tate I think you are, you'll put this (accident) behind you and pick up that horn." A nurse read the letter to Buddy, and he forced himself to return to playing.

I heard Buddy at a number of parties after he recovered from the accident. Although badly scarred, he performed beautifully. I especially liked a blues that Buddy composed called "Blue Creek," which he played on clarinet.

Buddy and Al Grey, *right,* were two of Count Basie's key sidemen. They went on together to break it up throughout the world during the '70s and '80s with "Jumpin' at the Woodside" and other Basie favorites. (St. Louis, 1984)

At the 1974 Colorado Springs party, I shot Buddy and Flip Phillips, *left,* two of the giants on tenor sax from the glory days of the big bands. It was fun watching them trying to outdo each other.

Buddy was playing with Jackie Williams, *left,* and Milt Hinton and Jay McShann when Cliff and Rene Leeman took Ann and me to Michael's Pub in New York in 1977. Upon spotting Cliff, Buddy introduced him and had the guys do an upbeat "Cherokee," which Cliff had played with Charlie Barnet years earlier.

Frank Tate

Frank has long been a first-call bass player in New York, but he started working the jazz party circuit some time after many other veteran musicians did. He has played in Pine Bluff with Ed Polcer, and I enjoy his quick wit and his stories of working with Dave McKenna, Billy Butterfield, and other favorite musicians of mine.

Earlier in his career, Frank played with Marion McPartland, the fine pianist who has contributed so much to jazz history with her *Piano Jazz* series on radio. He also accompanies the popular pianist-singer Bobby Short.

Frank, like Marty Grosz, has great rapport with the audience whenever he's called up for a feature number. At the March of Jazz party in Clearwater, Florida, Frank came on the stand to do a set with Daryl Sherman, another excellent singer and pianist. Daryl handed him a complicated bass part. Frank looked it over and jokingly protested that it was too difficult for him to read. Then they started to play and he cut it perfectly.

Frank is a fine bass player and a lot of fun to be around. As with Marty Grosz, the conversation never stops. That's drummer Wayne Jones in the background of this shot at the Atlanta party in 1995.

I took this picture right after Frank had played a particularly good solo. His expression shows his pleasure with the audience's reaction. (Waterloo Village, 1996)

When Frank's feature came up during a tour with a band led by Ed Polcer, he chatted with the audience. He is a great entertainer, and his patter had everyone in stitches. (Hot Springs, 1994)

Clark Terry

Clark is a powerful, inventive trumpet and flugelhorn player who starred in Duke Ellington's band before Dick Gibson ever thought about having a jazz party. I first heard him at the Gibson parties of the early '70s, and he soon became a regular at the Odessa parties as well.

In 1975, the first year that Ed Polcer played the Odessa party, I snapped a picture of him blowing his cornet with Clark at a local school where Milt Hinton had arranged for some of the musicians to perform for the kids. When I asked Ed to autograph the photo, he demonstrated the respect that brass players have for Clark. Ed wrote: "Al, thanks for capturing this once in a lifetime for me."

Clark has delighted audiences for years with his vocal feature, a blues called "Mumbles," on which he scats unintelligible lyrics that sound as though they make perfect sense. In another specialty, he holds his trumpet in one hand and his flugelhorn in the other—and plays alternate fours with himself.

Clark brings cheers from audiences with "Mumbles," a blues vocal in which he scats unintelligible lyrics. On the flag-waving out chorus, he plays trumpet with his left hand and fluglehorn with his right, as shown here. (Colorado Springs, 1978)

Clark was one of Duke Ellington's most famous sidemen. His personality reflects his great sense of humor and makes him one of the leading spokesmen of jazz. (Colorado Springs, 1978)

This photo of Clark and Ed Polcer, *right,* was taken at a school during the 1975 Odessa party. Playing with Clark was a "once in a lifetime" for Ed, as he wrote in his inscription. Clark is always willing to perform for schoolkids.

Allan Vaché

Allan's obbligato work on clarinet makes him a great asset in the front line of a traditional jazz band. He was featured in Jim Cullum's band for seventeen years. Allan turned out some fine work on the band's records and on its National Public Radio program.

Like his older brother, Warren, a marvelous cornetist, Allan is an extremely versatile player. And like Kenny Davern, he has great range on clarinet. In fact, Kenny taught him the fingering for those extra high notes.

Allan gave Ann and me a wonderful surprise years ago when we took a trip to San Antonio, the home base of the Cullum band. We arrived on a Sunday afternoon, and I called Allan. I knew that the band would be off that night, but Allan said never mind. He told us to go to the Landing, where the band plays regularly. Allan said that Jack Wyatt, Jim's bass player, would be fronting a group featuring the veteran clarinetist Herb Hall. As soon as Ann and I walked into the club, out came Allan with his horn. He spent more than two hours on his night off playing lovely duets with Herb.

Allan's performances on clarinet are pure excitement. The younger brother of Warren, he starred in the Jim Cullum Jazz Band for seventeen years. (Pine Bluff, 1995)

Herb Hall, *left,* and Allan played beautiful duets for Ann and me on a Sunday night at the Landing, Jim Cullum's club. It was Allan's night off, but he came down and did three sets with Herb and a rhythm section. (San Antonio, 1986)

Allan sat in with Pee Wee Erwin, *left,* and Bobby Gordon, *right,* one night at Condon's in 1978. He and his dad, Warren Vaché, Sr.,
the bass player and jazz writer, came to the club and played with the regular band. Allan took Bobby's place with Jim Cullum.

Warren Vaché, Jr.

Warren is an exceptionally gifted cornet player who can do just about anything he wants to do on his horn. He puts more beauty into a ballad than any other cornet or trumpet player I've ever heard. Like Randy Sandke, when Warren goes for one of those extremely high or low notes, he usually nails it.

I met Warren when Pee Wee Erwin brought him to Pine Bluff in 1978 to play in the band for my 50th birthday party. Pee Wee had been Warren's cornet teacher and had worked with his father, Warren Vaché, Sr., who plays bass. Warren's weekend in Pine Bluff was very painful. My son, Al III, took him to see his horse, which immediately stepped on Warren's foot.

One of the highlights of Warren's career was his association with Rosemary Clooney, along with Scott Hamilton, when they recorded several fine albums of standards for Concord. Warren was also featured in one of Benny Goodman's last bands.

Warren's younger brother, Allan, a superb clarinetist, tells about the band fronted by Walt Levinsky, whose trumpet section was made up of Randy Sandke, Spanky Davis, and Warren. The other musicians called the section Sandke, Spanky, and Cranky.

Warren is a marvelous cornetist who puts extraordinary beauty into ballads. Although not particularly known for his singing, he does a heartfelt job with "Nobody Knows," complete with sobbing. (Hoboken, 1995)

Warren had an incomparable cornet teacher, Pee Wee Erwin, *left*. The two of them, shown here with Cliff Leeman, worked out some wonderful duets. (Jackson, Mississippi, 1978)

When I took this picture of Warren and Ed Polcer, *left,* at the 1996 Odessa party, they were playing "Buddy Bolden's Blues," Pee Wee Erwin's favorite tune. It brought tears to the eyes of everyone in the audience who had known Pee Wee, to whom Warren and Ed dedicated the number.

Johnny Varro

Front-line instrumentalists would name Johnny among their top choices to be on piano behind them. This pleasant, easygoing man has a casual way of playing that matches his personality. Johnny uses a fast, distinctive tremolo that seems to spread all over the piano.

As a young player, Johnny had the good fortune of knowing and learning from Willie the Lion Smith. The Lion's "Echo of Spring" has always been part of his solo repertoire. Johnny became a buddy of Pee Wee Erwin's when they played together at Nick's in New York. He later succeeded Ralph Sutton as intermission pianist at Condon's.

Johnny wrote all the excellent arrangements for the band he fronted on an Arbors CD. The group had a front line of Randy Sandke, Dan Barrett, Phil Bodner, and Harry Allen; and Johnny, Frank Tate, and Joe Ascione in the rhythm section. They sounded more like a big band than a small one.

Johnny can do it all on piano, and he's also a fine arranger. The years of playing at Nick's and Condon's in New York as a young man shine through in his playing. (Odessa, 1992)

Johnny is one of the few musicians who have the ability to keep the excitement level growing higher and higher throughout any tune he plays. I shot him accompanying Kenny Davern, *left,* at Waterloo Village in 1996.

A great pianist is all that's needed for an evening of top-flight jazz. Contrary to Johnny's inscription about this "ungodly trio of piano players,"
here are three of the best: Johnny, Ralph Sutton, and Ray Sherman, *left to right.* (Odessa, 1990)

Joe Venuti

I first heard this legendary hot violinist play at Dick Gibson's jazz party in Vail, Colorado, in 1970. Joe was in his 70s, and I got the biggest kick watching the reaction of Bobby Hackett when he played. Joe thrilled everyone at the party with his playing, but especially Bobby.

I asked Joe to autograph a photo of himself that I had taken from some publication. He looked at it and started talking about Eddie Lang, the great guitar player who died in 1933, as though he had seen him only recently. The two jazz immortals had worked together frequently during the '20s.

Joe was an outlandish practical joker. He once sent Wingy Manone, the one-armed trumpet player, one cuff link for Christmas. On another occasion, Joe put out a call for every bass and tuba player in New York to meet at a certain time on a certain corner. He watched from a hotel room as the musicians lugged their large, heavy instruments to the designated spot—and stood there looking at one another. Joe paid them scale for that stunt.

When I knew Joe, he was much more reserved but could still play up a storm. He had an arrangement of "Sweet Georgia Brown" at a fast tempo on which he played all four strings at once. Joe recorded prolifically during the '20s and '30s. He made some fine recordings late in life with Zoot Sims, the great tenor sax star.

I will always be grateful for the chance to have met and heard this fabulous musician who played such a major role in the history of jazz.

Joe was a master of jazz excitement on the violin from his days with Bix Beiderbecke and Eddie Lang in the '20s until his death in 1978. At the Colorado Springs party in 1975, he played a set with Larry Ridley and Bobby Rosengarden, *left and right*.

At Dick Gibson's 1970 party in Vail, Joe posed in front of Carl Fontana, Lou McGarity, harmonica player Toots Thelman, and Vic Dickenson, *left to right*. Joe's career got a new boost after he performed with musicians such as these.

It's easy to see why this band brought the crowd to its feet for a standing ovation. The players included, *left to right,* Joe Venuti, Larry Ridley, Flip Phillips, Peanuts Hucko, Bobby Rosengarden, and Red Norvo. Joe and Red played together with Paul Whiteman in the '20s. (Colorado Springs, 1975)

Dick Wellstood

I first heard Dick at the Gibson party at the Broadmoor Hotel in Colorado Springs in 1973. Pee Wee Erwin introduced him and told the audience, "Dick will play you a solo that you cannot refuse." And did he ever, romping through James P. Johnson's classic "Carolina Shout."

Dick played piano in the Wildcats, the teenage band formed by Bob Wilber. As a young man, he idolized Joe Sullivan, the intermission pianist at Eddie Condon's club. Dick went to Condon's and other jazz joints wearing a sign on his lapel—and handing out business cards—that read, "Maybe you can help me meet Joe Sullivan, my name is Dick Wellstood."

Charoscuro issued an LP called *Dick Wellstood and His Famous Orchestra Featuring Kenny Davern.* That's what it says on the front cover. The back cover says *All Star* instead of *Famous.* Either way, the orchestra consists of Kenny on soprano sax and Dick on piano. They changed the title of one of the tunes. Duke Ellington's "Jubilee Stomp" became "Fast As a Bastard." William F. Buckley, Jr., wrote the clever liner notes.

Dick always said that jazz should be played with a little grease and funk. He had a clean, firm touch on the keyboard, but the grease and funk were always there. Dick died of a heart attack in his hotel room at the beginning of the 1987 Peninsula party in Palo Alto. He left an abundant legacy of recordings, but I miss him and I miss hearing live performances of the grease and funk that gave his playing such a great sense of humor. Ralph Sutton nicknamed him "Wellstride."

Dick's engaging personality is portrayed nicely in his biography, *Giant Strides,* by Edward N. Meyer.

Dick had just finished playing a terrific version of James P. Johnson's "Carolina Shout" when I took this picture. His expression shows that he was pleased with his performance and so was the audience. (Colorado Springs, 1973)

Dick and Kenny Davern, *left,* were close friends and made some great recordings together during the '70s. Dick suffered a fatal heart attack at the 1987 Peninsula party in Palo Alto, and Kenny had the painful task of identifying his body. (Wilmington, 1982)

This shot of Dick at the piano was taken in my living room. Ann had told him that she loved the tune "Memory" from the musical *Cats*, and Dick was learning it from the sheet music. (Pine Bluff, 1984)

Bob Wilber

Bob is an excellent reed player, performing primarily on clarinet and soprano sax. He also has had a remarkable career as an arranger and composer. While in high school, Bob formed a band called the Wildcats, whose members included Eddie Hubble and Dick Wellstood. Later, Bob studied with Sidney Bechet and lived in the master's home while learning from him.

Bob played at Eddie Condon's club, and I love the recordings he made with Wild Bill Davison and Cutty Cutshall. He also played with Bobby Hackett's combo and many other groups featuring the elite of jazz. When Dick Gibson turned the Ten Greats of Jazz into the World's Greatest Jazz Band, Bob replaced Peanuts Hucko.

At the 1972 Gibson party, Dick asked Kenny Davern and Bob to play a soprano sax duet. The audience went wild as the two of them hit the final notes of "The Mooche." Thus was born Soprano Summit, one of the outstanding jazz combos of all time.

Bob also created the Bechet Legacy, a combo that specialized in the music of his early teacher. The group featured singer Joanne (Pug) Horton, Bob's wife. Assisted by Derek Webster, Bob wrote a candid autobiography called *Music Was Not Enough*.

When I took this picture, Bob was playing clarinet and soprano sax with the World's Greatest Jazz Band and they had unexpectedly taken the stage in their traveling clothes at Dick Gibson's Labor Day party. As a teenager, Bob lived in the home of his teacher, the great Sidney Bechet. (Colorado Springs, 1973)

Dick Gibson called Bob's curved soprano sax a "toy sax." Pee Wee Erwin considered Bob and Kenny Davern the two best clarinetists. He complained that they were playing "fish horns" when they switched to soprano sax. (Colorado Springs, 1976)

In 1973, Bob and Kenny Davern, *left*, formed Soprano Summit, a five-piece band that made some of the finest recordings I have ever heard. These two masters play together magnificently, producing an incomparable blend of sound. (St. Louis, 1994)

Joe Wilder

Joe plays beautiful trumpet and flugelhorn, and he ranks up there with George Masso as the Mr. Nice Guy of jazz. Joe also follows Bobby Hackett's example in having difficulty saying anything nasty about anyone or anything.

For years, the Conneaut Lake jazz party in Pennsylvania was held in a very old hotel. The rooms had antique plumbing and iron beds, and a single bare light bulb hung from the ceiling. During a set with Joe, Dan Barrett announced a tune by Bix Beiderbecke and told the audience, "I think I'm staying in Bix's room." Marty Grosz then went into one of his spiels and talked about having a tour of the rooms the next morning. When Joe's turn came, he said only, "Well, I guess they could fix it up a little."

Like Milt Hinton, Joe is an excellent photographer. We always take pictures of each other at parties and swap them.

Joe and George Masso get my vote as Mr. Nice Guy among the musicians I have met. Like all the other great jazz players, Joe has his own easily recognizable sound. Ballads have a special beauty coming out of his trumpet. (Conneaut Lake, 1984)

Joe posed with me when Ann and I saw the musical *42nd Street* in New York in 1984. Bob Haggart had told us that Joe was in the pit band, so we went down and chatted. Joe met Ann and me after the show and stayed with us in a driving rain until we could get a cab back to our hotel.

The audience at the 1984 Conneaut Lake party heard a trio of fine trumpet players when Joe teamed up with Ed Polcer, *left,* and Dick Cathcart, *right.* Joe is also a master on flugelhorn.

Jackie Williams

Jackie is an extremely tasty drummer, never too loud or overbearing, but just loud enough to move the front line. He is very popular at jazz parties and has worked in all the New York night spots for almost half a century. Laurie Wright, the editor of *Storyville* magazine, called Jackie "one of the few really thoughtful and tasteful drummers."

I first heard this soft-spoken, friendly little man when Cliff and Rene Leeman took Ann and me to Michael's Pub in the summer of 1977. Jackie still impresses me with the solid sound of his sock cymbal, which a drummer operates with the left foot. I also like what he does on a solo using only his hands on the snare drum.

Dan Barrett and Howard Alden selected Jackie as drummer for their fine combo, the Alden-Barrett Quintet. He also was a member of Doc Cheatham's Sunday afternoon band at Sweet Basil's in New York. During the '70s and '80s, Jackie played with Ed Polcer at Condon's.

When Jackie played at Condon's, he often teamed with Jack Lesberg, *right,* in the rhythm section. Jackie once asked me to make some glossy photos for him for publicity purposes. I am pleased to have been able to help a lot of jazz artists in this small way. (New York, 1978)

Howard Alden and Dan Barrett chose Jackie on drums when they formed their fine little band, the ABQ. This photo shows him playing a solo on the snare drum with only his hands. (Hoboken, 1995)

Jackie is one of the great timekeeping drummers who has worked with all the top jazz musicians in and around New York. The word "tasty" describes his playing perfectly. (St. Petersburg, 1994)

Chuck Wilson

Chuck is a fine reed player who is featured in Howard Alden and Dan Barrett's excellent combo, the ABQ. He gives the Alden-Barrett Quintet a full sound and stands out on a number of arrangements and original compositions written by the great Buck Clayton a few years before his death. The group's recording of "Night in Tunisia," featuring Chuck on clarinet, is a special favorite of mine.

I've heard Chuck play clarinet and alto sax at jazz parties in Conneaut Lake, Waterloo Village, and Clearwater. In addition to his natural feeling for jazz, Chuck is a fine reader. At the Clearwater party, Dan handed him an arrangement that he had just written for vocalist Becky Kilgore. Chuck had it cold the first time through.

Chuck has been the reed player in the ABQ since Howard Alden, *left,* and Dan Barrett started the combo. His clarinet and alto sax create a beautiful blend of sound with Dan and Howard. (Hoboken, 1995)

This photo shows Jack Lesberg, Scott Robinson, Dan Barrett, and Chuck, *left to right,* playing behind a Becky Kilgore vocal at the 1996 Clearwater party. They were reading the arrangements Dan wrote for Becky's *I Saw Stars* CD.

Chuck plays a lovely clarinet solo with the ABQ on Dizzy Gillespie's "Night in Tunisia." I snapped Howard Alden, Frank Tate, Chuck, and Dan Barrett, *left to right,* at the 1996 March of Jazz in Clearwater.

Teddy Wilson

I first saw Teddy in person at the first Dick Gibson party that Robert Nixon and I went to, in 1970 in Vail, Colorado. Teddy didn't show up on the opening night. He had played in a jam session in Denver the night before and had too much to drink. When he woke up, he called Dick and told him, "I'm looking at my watch and it says ten o'clock, but I don't know if that's a.m. or p.m."

Teddy played the Odessa party several times and sounded just like he did on all the great recordings I had heard him on through the years. He was a bright, sincere man and told me about teaching at the Juilliard School in New York. One of his students was pop pianist Roger Williams. Teddy said Roger lacked a natural feeling for jazz, and they spent hours playing duets in an effort to teach him jazz timing.

Red Norvo and his wife, singer Mildred Bailey, gave a party one night, and the guests included Teddy and Benny Goodman. Mildred asked them to play together with her cousin, Carl Bellinger, an amateur drummer. Thus was born the idea of the Benny Goodman Trio, one of the immortal combos of jazz.

Two Dutch jazz fans, Arie Ligthart and Humphrey van Loo, worked with Teddy on his autobiography, *Teddy Wilson Talks Jazz*. Benny wrote the foreword, which begins: "This is a foreword, but not an introduction, because Teddy Wilson does not need one."

Teddy was playing solo piano in the famous Bemelman's Bar in New York's Carlyle Hotel when I took this photo in 1978. I have loved his playing since I was about ten years old and heard Mildred Bailey's 1935 record of "Downhearted Blues," featuring Teddy, Bunny Berigan, and Johnny Hodges.

Four of my favorite jazzmen posed together at the 1983 Odessa party. Teddy stood behind Flip Phillips and between Dave McKenna, *left,* and Milt Hinton.

Teddy and Pee Wee Erwin flanked me in this shot at the Odessa party in 1977. If you can find a copy of *The Otis Ferguson Reader,* read what that eminent critic had to say in the '30s about Teddy.

Kai Winding

Kai was a trombonist with whom I swapped trousers when he played a gig with the World's Greatest Jazz Band. The band had a date in Memphis in 1970, and Kai, subbing for Carl Fontana, didn't have the group's uniform. Dick Gibson, sponsor of the WGJB spotted my dark trousers, and I lent them to Kai. I had to stand up for the whole concert because Kai was at least three inches smaller in the waist.

Kai was born in Denmark, and his family moved to the United States when he was twelve years old. He started to play trombone at the age of fifteen and was performing professionally full time by the time he was eighteen. Kai worked for Benny Goodman in the mid-'40s, but his big break came when he joined Stan Kenton in 1947. Kenton gave him lots of solos, and Kai received much public attention.

In 1954, Kai formed a fine quintet with another top trombonist, J.J. Johnson. After that group disbanded, he organized a highly successful septet with four trombones and a rhythm section.

I first heard Kai at the Gibson party in Vail, Colorado, in 1970. At one of the Odessa parties, Pee Wee Erwin had an audition tape by a young woman piano player. Kai listened to it in my room and, completely voluntarily, wrote the nicest critique for her.

What a quartet this was! Kai, with a rhythm section of, *left to right*, Ralph Sutton, Milt Hinton, and Cliff Leeman, blew away the audience at the Odessa party in 1974.

Kai huddled with two other top trombonists, Carl Fontana and Urbie Green, *left and center*, to work out an on-the-spot arrangement at the 1971 Colorado Springs party.

Kai was one of the great jazz soloists from the Big Band Era, especially with Stan Kenton. He's shown here with Bucky Pizzarelli, *center,* and Herb Ellis. (Odessa, 1975)

Trummy Young

Trummy was one of the great straight-ahead trombone players from the Big Band Era. His first major job came with Earl Hines, from 1934 to 1937, but he rose to stardom with Jimmie Lunceford, with whom he played from 1937 to 1943. Trummy joined Louis Armstrong's All Stars in 1953 and was featured throughout the world for twelve years.

Trummy's trombone solo on the Lunceford recording of "Margie" has been copied by virtually every trombonist. On the last beat he plays a high note on which he goes from first position to seventh, giving the effect of a fast full scale. He also contributed the vocal. Like almost all great jazz musicians, Trummy developed a distinctive sound on his instrument. I loved the way he played the blues, and his breathless vocal style.

I first heard Trummy at Dick Gibson's parties in Colorado Springs during the early '70s. He was always gracious to jazz fans. The last time I saw him, at the 1984 Peninsula Jazz Party in Menlo Park, California, he was especially nice to Barbara Sutton Curtis, an underrated pianist. Trummy gave Barbara, who is Ralph Sutton's sister, a feature on every set he led. He died at his home in Hawaii a few weeks after that party.

If you look closely, you can see the half-moon on Trummy's upper lip. It resulted from playing trombone all those years, especially with Jimmie Lunceford and Louis Armstrong. (Colorado Springs, 1976)

I've been a big fan of Trummy's since first hearing the wonderful Jimmie Lunceford record of "Margie." On it, Trummy sings his breathless vocal and then plays his famous trombone solo with the "rip" to the highest note on the horn at the end. (Colorado Springs, 1978)

Three of the greatest trombone players from the big bands played together at the 1973 Colorado Springs party. Trummy stood between Tyree Glenn, *left,* and Vic Dickenson, with Ray Brown on bass.

acknowledgments

I deeply appreciate the assistance of all those who had a part in putting this book together.

The first person I thank is my partner in the *Jazz Party* project, Jim Shacter. He and I talked for several years about creating a book of my photographs of jazz musicians. Jim agreed to provide the text of the book by editing the information I sent him about the musicians. The venture never would have gotten off the ground if he had not kept asking me when I planned to get started.

Thanks to Sandra M. Dyrlund for her expert counsel in selecting the pictures we used. I took more than 3,000 of my favorite photos to Chicago, and Sandra worked with Jim and me for three days picking the best ones.

The format of *Jazz Party* was inspired by my friend Milt Hinton, the great bass player. Milt's excellent jazz photos in his two books *Bass Line* and *Over Time* made me think I could come up with a useful and entertaining volume. His collaborators, David G. Berger and Holly Maxson, David's photographer wife, came to Pine Bluff and spent a couple of days looking at my pictures and advising me about the possibility of doing this book. Thanks to Milt and his wife, Mona, and to David and Holly for their advice and support.

Of all the musicians I have known, Bob Haggart was my best friend. Bob's foreword to the book, written just weeks before his death, brings tears to my eyes.

Three other musicians who have died—Pee Wee Erwin, Yank Lawson, and Cliff Leeman—were close friends who shared a lot of personal jazz history with me.

Ed Polcer and his wife, Judy, are among those to whom I feel closest. Ed continually encouraged me to get the job done and gave me a lot of help. Other outstanding musicians who are close friends and candidly shared their thoughts and stories include Joe Ascione, Dan Barrett, Kenny Davern, Bobby Gordon, George Masso, Ken Peplowski, Randy Sandke, and Ralph Sutton.

Although a lot of fine musicians whom I have met during more than thirty years of attending jazz parties are not featured in this book, I appreciate their great talent and excellent performances.

Each of the individuals pictured in *Jazz Party* not only contributed to the project, but also provided tremendous personal pleasure by letting me see and hear America's only true art form up close and personal. Thanks to all of them. It's been a blast!

index